The Four Conversations

Daily Communication That Gets Results

By
Jeffrey Ford
Laurie Ford

16
EasyRead Large

Copyright Page from the Original Book

The Four Conversations

 Berrett-Koehler Publishers, Inc.
235 Montgomery Street, Suite 650
San Francisco, California 94104-2916
Tel: (415) 288-0260, Fax: (415) 362-2512
www.bkconnection.com

Ordering information for print editions
Quantity sales. Special discounts are available on quantity purchases by cor-
porations, associations, and others. For details, contact the "Special Sales
Department" at the Berrett-Koehler address above.
Individual sales. Berrett-Koehler publications are available through most
bookstores. They can also be ordered directly from Berrett-Koehler: Tel:
(800) 929-2929; Fax: (802) 864-7626; www.bkconnection.com
Orders for college textbook/course adoption use. Please contact Berrett-
Koehler: Tel: (800) 929-2929; Fax: (802) 864-7626.
Orders by U.S. trade bookstores and wholesalers. Please contact Ingram
Publisher Services, Tel: (800) 509-4887; Fax: (800) 838-1149; E-mail:
customer.service@ingrampublisherservices.com; or visit www.ingram
publisherservices.com/Ordering for details about electronic ordering.

First Edition
Paperback print edition ISBN 978-1-57675-920-2
PDF e-book ISBN 978-1-57675-921-9

2009-1

Interior production by Publication Services. Cover design by Richard Adelson.

TABLE OF CONTENTS

More Praise for The Four Conversations

"This work by Jeffrey and Laurie Ford is compelling. While there is much literature on the content of effective management—the concepts, models, vocabulary, and acronyms—there is almost nothing on the conversational competence essential to being an effective manager, leader, or executive. Recognizing and being adept with these four conversations is crucial for anyone who aspires to effective management."

—Brian Stuhlmuller, Partner, Distinctions, Inc., and former CEO, Mission Control Productivity, Inc., and MediMedia Information Technologies

"I've got nothing but praise for this book. Literally, from beginning to end, I was impressed with the concrete, real-life scenarios the authors used to demonstrate their points. This is good, solid material, presented in a way that clearly communicates the value of using four types of conversations consciously and deliberately. As a manager myself, I've got an initiative conversation in mind for my next weekly staff meeting."

—Chris Lee, Editor, *Midwest Home* magazine, and former Editor-in-Chief, *Training* magazine

"*The Four Conversations* offers insight and clarity about the way we speak to one another. Its perceptive observations and real-life examples are valuable in enhancing daily communication with friends and family and indispensable to anyone attempting transformative change."

—Cheryl Roberto, Commissioner, Public Utilities Commission of Ohio

"This book captures the critical elements of meaningful workplace conversation in a way that will help managers communicate more effectively. *The Four Conversations* is filled with examples that will improve both performance and engagement."

—Cindy Ventrice, author of *Make Their Day! Employee Recognition That Works*

To our
students and clients,
from whom we have learned so much.

Preface

As a management professor and management consultant, we have had the opportunity to work, train, and problem-solve with executives and managers in nearly every type of organization, from small businesses and Fortune 100 companies to nonprofits, associations, and government agencies at the city, state, and federal levels. The most frequently cited challenge, beyond all others, is "communication." Over the last twenty-five years of teaching and consulting, we have discovered two things about the communication problem in organizations.

First, most people do not know that communication is actually made up of different types of conversations. People think of communication as a broad general area riddled with problems, gaps, and pitfalls in which success is a matter of skill or luck or both. Unfortunately, this generalization is like saying "I have a driving problem, " when one needs to start by learning the difference between ignition, steering wheel, accelerator, and brake. Generalizations do not solve the very real problems of organizational work.

Second, most people do not understand that his or her own communication, not someone else's, is the key to recognizing and resolving the communication problem. It is easy to blame others, either individually or as a group, for not communicating well. Now we need to consider that

Research at the Harvard Business School indicates that 70% of all organizational changes fail to produce their intended results.[1] Communication is usually the designated culprit in these failures. Why, then, if everyone knows communication is so important, have we not solved the problem? Perhaps seeing it as a generic problem, caused by other people or environmental factors, has limited our vision. As individuals, each of us has our own pattern of daily conversations, and we can learn to change that pattern. This means we can alter our conversational habits, and start communicating more effectively.

There are four types of conversation, each with a set of necessary elements. They are normal everyday conversations, used by CEOs, executives, directors, managers, supervisors, and employees (and husbands and wives, parents and children) in the process of doing their respective jobs. Anyone who wants to accomplish something, whether creating a new corporate strategy, assigning people to projects, or arranging lunch with friends, will use one or more of these four conversations.

When our students and clients began to practice improving their skills with all four conversations in their work situations, they were amazed to discover how very small changes in the way they talked could produce unexpectedly positive outcomes. Practicing managers were impressed with how easy it was to get results, and quickly applied the lessons to get similar benefits outside of work with spouses, families, and friends.

We have since learned many of the persistent issues people tolerate in organizations can be resolved by using these four conversations. True, some people do not want to change the way they communicate or do not want to make changes in their work practices. However, we have found most people are willing to make minor adjustments in their speaking and listening to gain major improvements in results and relationships.

The material developed in this book reflects what we have learned from research and consulting with executives and managers, training them in MBA and executive education classes, and solving problems in their organizations. We have included many of their stories and experiences, as well as first-hand observations, to give examples of how people changed their conversations and what happened as a result. The people and the examples are real, though we have altered the names of individuals and organizations.

We wrote this book to give executives, managers, and employees—and their families and friends—a way to overcome communication problems every day, in every conversation. We explain the four types of conversations, including the required elements in each, and the specific kinds of results each conversation can produce. Examples of real conversations and results are included throughout.

The book starts in Chapter 1 by addressing the daily and persistent problems we encounter at work and how they can be addressed by recognizing four different types of conversations.

Chapter 2 introduces Initiative Conversations, useful whenever you want to propose something new, make something happen, or create a new future. Chapter 3 presents Understanding Conversations, which you can use to engage other people in planning and participating in your goals. Chapter 4 is about Performance Conversations, the little-used rules for creating commitment, getting people to move into action, and producing results. Chapter 5 describes Closure Conversations, the often-overlooked key to accomplishment, satisfaction, and accountability.

In Chapter 6, you will see how to put the four types of conversation together in different ways to accomplish different objectives, including ways to expand your personal effectiveness, enhance other people's performance, and improve relationships. Each section in the chapter includes tips, tested by practicing managers, for stimulating better communi-cation, productivity, and workplace satisfaction.

Chapter 7 outlines some ways to change conversa-tional patterns in a work environment. It contains ideas from managers on how to support new ways of talking at work, such as how to have better meetings, and some tips to help you practice and get other people to practice with you. A closing note reminds us that changing our conversations will change more than the way we speak. It will change our listening too, so that we will be more responsive to, and perhaps more responsible for, our human environment.

Chapter One

Four Conversations in a Successful Workplace

Realizing your goals will take more than passion, vision, and commitment: it will take talking to other people. To be successful, your talking must accomplish more than simply following the rules of well-mannered communication skills. Getting more of what you want and less of what you don't want—in work and in life—depends on how well you use four types of conversations.

1. ***Initiative Conversations:*** When you talk in a way that proposes something new or different, such as introducing a new goal, proposing an idea, or launching a change in strategy or structure, you are having an Initiative Conversation.

     Example: You are a manager who announces a new customer service policy. Your announcement can be done in a way that attracts people toward working with you to implement the new policy, or it can be so vague or bossy that everyone goes back to doing their own work, leaving you to wonder how you will do it all yourself.

2.

     Example: You explain the purpose of your new customer service policy and your plan for its implementation, and encourage people to make suggestions and contribute their advice. The way you talk will either help people see how to support you or create confusion and annoyance.

3. ***Performance Conversations:*** When you want people to take specific actions or produce specific results, you make specific requests (and promises) so they know what to do and when to do it. Performance Conversations, when properly conducted, will lead people to work, perform tasks, and produce results.

    Example: You are a manager who directs all employees to follow the new customer service policy starting today (your request) and asks for a show of hands (their promise) by everyone who accepts the request. This establishes an agreement for action. Your request could be so effective that people start to implement it that afternoon, or so sketchy it leaves people unsure about what you really want, when you want it, and whether it really matters.

4. ***Closure Conversations:*** When you thank someone for his or her work, summarize the status of a project, or tell people that a job is complete, you are having a Closure Conversation.

The Importance of Conversations

Everything we talk about involves one or more of the four types of conversation. We use them when we are socializing, talking about the weather, discussing the big game, or chatting about an upcoming party. We use them when we are learning about the computer system, getting assignments from the boss, or explaining how the travel policy works to a new employee. Any time we are trying to motivate people, get them to be more productive, or help them solve a problem, we are using one or more of these four conversations.

At work, managers introduce ideas and improvements. They want to have people understand, take appropriate action, and create an environment of teamwork and communication. The problem is that many managers make mistakes in the way they use these conversations, or leave out important parts that help get the message across.

Abraham was a supervisor in a fast-growing organization where staff turnover was unusually high. Both the rapid growth and the high turnover increased Abraham's workload to the point where he was working longer days and weekends, much to the disappointment of his family. He knew he was in a negative cycle, doing more work himself and reducing the amount of time to train staff and be a good supervisor, but he was unable to turn the situation around.

"I talked to my supervisor about it, " Abraham said. "He agreed the staff shortage was a problem. He knows I am working too many hours, and that I'm unhappy about it. But he has not done anything to resolve the problem. Maybe he doesn't care."

We asked Abraham about the details of his conversations with his boss, and he told us, "My boss and I agreed that our staff turnover meant we have to spend more time training new people, and the increase in customers also increases our work, "Abraham said. "We talked about why the workload has gone up, and then we shared some personal stories about how we cope with the effects on our family life. It's hard for him too. We agreed that something should be done, but we aren't sure what."

Abraham and his boss had an Understanding Conversation. Neither of them used an Initiative Conversation to propose a solution, or a Performance Conversation to request a change of some kind. When he learned about Performance Conversations, Abraham decided to be bold. He went to his boss with some new requests for action.

"I asked him to look into his budget, " Abraham said, "and see if he could either hire two new people or get two temps in here right away. I also asked him to give me permission to stop working overtime in the evenings and weekends, starting now. And I asked him for a week's vacation before the end of the month. I told him I needed to get reacquainted with my family."

"I never got the vacation, " he said later, "but I did get all my weekends off starting that week.

My boss contacted a key customer and changed four deadlines we had promised for customer deliveries. He asked for two new hires, and we actually got one of them, which is a miracle. These were great results for me and I feel better about working here. The most important thing I learned, though, is that talking

We all have habitual ways of conversing with people around us. In our collaboration with hundreds of practicing managers, most were surprised to learn how frequently they used each type of conversation, and how and why they used them. Many saw that they were indirect, and only hinted at what they wanted other people to do. Some made clear requests to some of their colleagues or friends but not to others, or explained *why*they wanted something, but never got to the point of giving a clear instruction. Some went out of their way to show appreciation, while others rarely said "good job, " or "thank you" to the people who worked with them.

We all know that we do not talk the same way to our boss as we do with our spouse, children, or friends. But do you know *what*is different? Do you use all four types of conversation with skill and ease? Or do you use one or two conversations most of the time, and other ones only rarely?

If you are getting what you want in most areas of your life, and the people around you are supporting your goals, you are probably using all four types of conversations skillfully. If not, it may be time to update your patterns of talk. Too often, when we fail to get what we want, we blame other factors such as authority, personality, or motives. We can choose an alternative and look to our own way of talking to see how it affects our relationships and results. For example, Abraham blamed his boss for not caring about his problem of overwork. When he learned new ways to change his conversation, he got a better outcome than he expected.

Some Conversations Slow Things Down, Others Speed Things Up

Many of our conversations seem to make no difference. Office meetings can be "too much talking with nothing happening." Some conversations slow our progress by distracting us from important issues or giving us irrelevant information that only adds confusion. Other conversations, however, give us insight into solving a problem, or provide fresh direction and clarity. When we have a goal or a desire to accomplish something, some conversations will be productive, and others will not.

Unproductive Conversations

Complaints are an example of conversations that are usually unproductive. When people complain about the weather, such as, "It always rains when I want to play golf, " they say it with no intention to change the weather, or even, at that moment, to move to a drier climate or buy a rain suit and adapt.

Many complaints at work are like complaints about the weather. People do not intend to do anything to resolve the complaint, and often have no solutions in mind. Even where solutions exist, or could be developed, the complainer does not intend to be the one who will push for implementing them. Complaints about anything—the weather or a problem at work or at home—which lack a commitment to create or work toward a solution, are simply a distraction to everyone within earshot. Uncommitted complaints are unproductive conversations, and have a negative effect on morale and performance.

We have seen brainstorming sessions, however, that sounded like a lot of complaining, but produced valuable outcomes. Participants itemized all the things wrong with their Four Conversations in a Successful Workplace 7 organization, systems, or policies, but they were actually working to find the underlying causes of negative situations and invent better ways to get things done. Their outcome was a list of solutions—the product of a commitment to make improvements.

The difference between productive and unproductive complaints is a matter of *intention.* Do the people involved in the conversation have any intention to take actions that will resolve the complaint? If not, the conversation is not a productive one to engage in.

Blaming is another popular, but unproductive, conversation. When we talk about who or what is the cause of a problem, we may want to blame "them, " those wrongdoers who have made—or failed to make—decisions or actions. Who did it? "They" did. We blame them because "they" do not understand, are incompetent, or have a selfish hidden agenda.

Complaining and blaming both take up time and energy but do not change anything for the better. In fact, by engaging in conversations about the culprits and their wrongdoings, we may contribute to a general sense of helplessness. Whether the conversation is about the boss's poor leadership, the negative effects of an office policy, or employee resistance to change, when we have no intention to find and implement a cure, we are merely fanning the flames of workplace resentment and frustration. As these negative sentiments build, people become more resigned and cynical, reducing their chances of winning either personal or professional success.

Gossip, or passing along negative stories and comments about other people, is also unproductive, and sometimes damaging to both the participants and the subject of the gossip. Although people may use gossip as a way of being more personally related to one another, it is at best a distraction from, or an avoidance of, productive work. It also undermines the credibility of the subject, and, less obviously, it undermines the trustworthiness of the gossiper. A person who tells you something negative about someone else can be expected to do the same to you behind your back.

Unproductive conversations—complaints, blaming, and gossip—will probably always exist in organizations and communities. It is useful, however, to realize when they are not productive. You can add intention and use of the four conversations to restore integrity and promote performance that will be more positive for everyone involved.

Four Productive Conversations

Each of the four conversations has a different purpose, and produces a different kind of result or impact on the listener. Used at the right times, and in the right combinations or patterns, these conversations can speed things up, add accountability, and reduce misunderstandings.

- **Initiative Conversations** share new ideas, goals, visions, and futures with people who can participate in implementing and making them real
- **Understanding Conversations** build awareness and knowledge of a new or existing idea in a way that helps people see how to participate in using or accomplishing it
-
- **Closure Conversations** support experiences of accomplishment, satisfaction, and value; strengthen accountability; and give people an honest look at the successes and failures encountered on the way to reaching a goal

Most of us want to be better at initiating things, getting people to understand our message, promoting effective action, and completing things. Now you can develop mastery in using the four conversations to produce results. Start by learning which conversations you are using, whether you are using the best one(s) for your purposes, and how to include all the components that will engage others in the ways you want.

Missing Conversations

The four types of conversations get things done, and build more productive and respectful relationships, but not everybody uses them in the same way. Most people are very successful with some types of conversation and less adept with others. Many people do not use all four types of conversation, either because they do not know there are other types of conversation that they could use, or because they choose not to use them. Our "missing conversations" can compromise the quality, timeliness, or participation in whatever we are doing, and sometimes even reduce our credibility and relatedness with staff and coworkers.

Jason is a mid-level manager accountable for two different installation projects in a communications company. Project A was progressing well, but Project B was three weeks behind schedule and regularly missing deadlines. Since the same people were involved in both projects, Jason's explanation for 10 The Four Conversations the problem was that his team members were not working well together on the two installations, and he needed more budget resources. "People problems and money problems, " he said. "Those are always the culprits."

To test his assumptions, Jason kept a project journal for one week, making detailed notes of what was said in his conversations with people about both projects. He also reviewed his emails and meeting summaries to take note of his conversational patterns. He expected to see a lot of talk about personnel and resource issues, but after reviewing his conversational records, he came to a different conclusion about the problems of Project B.

"The difference in my communications in the two projects was surprising, " he explained. "In Installation Project A, I asked for new ideas from my team members, explored ideas with everyone, and then we all made agreements about what we would do before our next meeting. In every weekly project meeting, we reviewed what had happened since our last meeting, did post-mortems on things that didn't go as expected, and then decided what we should do next."

"But, in Project B, I didn't do all that. The reason is that I have done the B-type installation before. I know how it should go, so I just explained to everybody what needed to be done instead of asking for their ideas and input. I gave people their assignments, and expected them to do their work. I was confident that these are capable people, so I didn't follow up with them."

Jason's review of Project B conversations showed he was missing Initiative Conversations (soliciting new ideas), Understanding Conversations (making sure people had a chance to interact about what needed to be done), and Closure Conversations (following up with his team on what was and was not accomplished). He decided to change his conversational pattern by talking with his Project B team about how to make the installation more successful and instituting a weekly follow-up meeting where team members could acknowledge work that was completed, what they had learned, and what remained to be done.

The first result he noticed was improved creativity and collaboration among the team members. The next was that productivity picked up. Five weeks later, Jason reported that his new conversational pattern had gotten Project B back on schedule.

Initiative Conversations. Some people do not set goals for themselves or their group, or, if they do, believe there is no need to communicate them to others. One executive explained, "People should know their jobs, and their jobs don't change just because I am setting a new goal for our division. If people need to alter their responsibilities, I will talk with them about it. I don't want to give a big speech, or publicly commit my whole division to a particular vision."

This particular executive was in a rapidly changing organization that was struggling to respond to major shifts in its own product technology and its industry's economic position. It was understandable that he did not want to "commit his whole division" to one goal, preferring to keep people focused on the familiar. At the same time, he was disappointed in his people's ability to be more creative in solving problems, and to collaborate across functional groups for creating what he called "new efficiencies."

This executive did not connect his lack of Initiative Conversations with the lack of creative thinking and teamwork. When he finally agreed to try them, he held an all-staff meeting and told everyone his top two strategies for surviving the organization's current risk position. Then he told them that he wanted all employees to stay focused on their jobs while also looking for opportunities to "find new solutions to old problems."

Several of the meeting participants mentioned later that they were glad to have a "bigger conversa-tion" than just the day-to-day routine. The executive was pleased to see a new spirit. "It's like everybody's sense of humor came back, " he said. "It looks like Initiative Conversations create a little more confidence in the future, and that's what we needed here now."

Understanding Conversations. Some people do not invite input and discussion after they unveil a new idea, goal, or plan. "Why do we need to explain the details?" one manager asked. "Everybody knows the goals here, since they are posted on our intranet. People should take their assignments and do them, without having everyone waste time in a meeting to figure out what they're supposed to do." This manager was strong in setting goals (Initiative Conversations) and in giving people feedback on progress (Closure Conversations). But once the goals were set, he preferred to give his staff their individual work assignments, and he saw no point in holding a group conversation to hear employee questions or comments.

When this manager saw that having an Understanding Conversation might give his employees a chance to hear and learn from each other in new ways, he agreed to have several group meetings to discuss department goals. In each discussion, he focused on the current process they were using to develop customer proposals. He was pleased to discover his people had many ideas to improve both teamwork and their communication between teams.

"I thought I was going to be put on the spot to defend things, " he said after the second meeting. "But instead, the employees started talking to each other, and we listed problems and solutions on the board. Everybody jumped in to answer the questions. I should have done this long ago!"

Performance Conversations. This type of conversation is most often one of the weakest in communications. "I shouldn't have to ask people to do specific things, " one director said, explaining why she didn't use them. "My people are very experienced and know what is expected without being asked."

She was opposed to the specific requests-and-promises requirement of Performance Conversations, fearing it would "disempower" people and make the workplace seem "cold." Still, she also wanted people to have more respect for deadlines and budgets, and wanted her teams to be more effective in working together to assemble new editions of their organization's monthly publications. "Can't we work like a well-oiled machine without keeping track of every little thing?" she wondered.

This director called a meeting of all her team leaders to identify what she called the "top ten internal agreements we need to keep with each other." This started as an Understanding Conversation and led into the requests and promises of Performance Conversations. Her goal was to discover where her staff members thought they needed to spell out deadlines, communicate expenditures, and establish agreements between teams, and then have people commit to those agreements.

"We have five main teams in this organization, " she told the group. "We want to work together in a way that nobody is ever waiting for something from another team. Let's get ahead of the curve and really help each other be productive." The group created a list of fourteen items they said they needed to communicate more clearly. They called it their "Ask and Promise" list, and posted it by the conference room door as a reminder to make those specific requests and promises whenever they were needed.

"Just agreeing to ask for and promise specific times for people to deliver their magazine copy was a breakthrough, " said one team leader. "We have been trying to avoid being too businesslike here, but sometimes it causes delays and bad feelings. I'm glad we have an 'Ask and Promise' board, and we can add to it whenever we want. We've been focused on being nice instead of being productive. The surprise is that we are nicer when we're more in sync with each other."

Closure Conversations. These conversations are frequently among the missing because, as one chief operating officer (COO) put it, "They've already been through a difficult challenge to finish the project. Why make everybody go back through it again?" This COO had introduced a new system for communicating customer business information between his sales people and his technical service staff. If used properly, his internal document management system would help the sales reps inform the "techs, " who could then provide the right services to the customers, and prevent failures in meeting customer expectations.

The problem was that only some of the sales reps were reliably using the system, and most of the techs were reluctant to report the problem. "We don't want to point fingers, " said one tech. So the customer business information was not always reliable, and some customers did not receive what they expected.

In the face of internal disagreements, a Closure Conversation can clear the air. The COO called his three sales managers and two technical team leaders into a meeting. "We need to look at where we are with using our document management system, " he said. "Here are the facts." He listed the customer accounts that had a "gap in expectations" created by sales reps who were not putting complete information into the system. He said, "You are all bright and talented people. You know how to use a document management system and how to capture information. What is the problem here?"

He discovered a few issues that kept people from doing things properly. One sales rep had delegated the data entry job to someone who was savvier with computers than he was, and that person disregarded the instructions for using the system. Another entire sales team held an inaccurate belief about which data fields were their responsibility to fill in, believing the office administrator should complete some fields. Finally, almost all sales reps disliked the new system, saying, "We never had any input in the way this document management system was designed, and the format for the technical data doesn't fit the way we have been trained to sell our customer accounts."

The COO agreed with this last statement, saying, "Given how much we've spent on sales training, I can't believe I didn't have one of those Understanding

Conversations to get the sales team involved in the process of designing the data entry form for the system. No wonder the team wasn't using it. We're going to go back and get the team members engaged, and then have a sales meeting to review the form. We will make whatever changes in the document management system that they can give me a good reason for making."

This COO has a new awareness of Closure Conversations. He says, "We will debrief at the end of every project. We're going to have a monthly status review of progress toward goals. And we're going to have regular team evaluations. I can't believe we went eight months trying to get something to work when we could have solved it much sooner with a few Closure Conversations. It was an expensive lesson, but I've learned it well."

As long as we are in situations where the types of conversation we know best are effective, every-thing is fine, and we get what we want. But when our interactions are not successful, or do not produce the results we want, we may attribute the problem to something about "them" (the other person or group) or "it" (a specific situation or environment). The alternative is to learn to apply other types of conversation in some of those "stuck" or difficult situations.

Difficult Conversations

A difficult conversation is anything you find hard to talk about.[1] Examples of potentially difficult conversations include asking your boss for a raise, firing an employee, giving someone a performance review, publicly asking critical questions about a popular issue, giving a friend bad news, or calling someone to account for poor work. They can be unsettling because we do not know how we, or the other person, will respond, and we may be afraid of where the conversation could go. As a result, we may be unsure of ourselves and put off the conversations or not have them at all.

Tori was apprehensive about talking with one of her employees because her past conversations with him had not produced any improvement in his performance, and she was facing a performance review deadline.

"What am I going to say to him that I haven't already said?" she asked. "He's on probation, and if he doesn't improve I will have to fire him, which I really don't want to do if I can avoid it. I am at a loss about what to say, and I am not looking forward to talking with him."

After learning about the four types of conversation, Tori realized she had only used Understanding Conversations with this employee. She had repeatedly explained the need for him to improve the quality of his work, but had never reviewed with him the regional goals (Initiative Conversation). She also had not made specific requests and agreements for outcomes (Performance Conversations), or met with him to review his specific work practices and results and acknowledge him for what he did accomplish (Closure Conversations).

Tori decided to try a combination of Understanding and Closure Conversations. "I told him that I was sorry I hadn't made my conditions clear to him, " she said. "I apologized for the uncertainty we both had had for the past two months (Closure Conversation). Then I itemized the three attributes of his work that I was going to measure from now on and we talked about them (Understanding Conversation). He promised that he would change his work practices and focus on making a measurable impact on those measures (Performance Conversation). We agreed that we would review his performance on the measures every Friday and every Monday, just to gain some momentum (Closure Conversations). His performance began improving in the second week."

Some conversations are difficult because we do not know which type of conversation to have, or even that there are different types of conversation. This is what happened in Tori's case. Other conversations are difficult because we do not know all the elements of whichever type of conversation is critical for success.

Incomplete Conversations: The Conversational Elements

One way to make sure each type of conversation is used completely is to borrow a tip from journalism: ask the questions *Who, What, When, Where, Why,* and *How* to get as much information as possible. The trick is to use these questions in a way that supports each of the four conversations.

For each type of conversation, the questions *What-When-Why* go together, because they all focus on whatever it is that you want to accomplish or make happen:

- *What* are we trying to accomplish?
- *When* do we want to accomplish it?
- *Why* is this accomplishment important?

The other three questions—*Who-Where-How*—go together, because they all relate to the resources and methods involved to make it happen:

- *Who* is involved?
- *Where* will the resources come from?
- *How* will it get done?

If some of these vital pieces of information are left out, the conversation is incomplete and even potentially productive conversations can slow people down or fail to engage them. Consider four managers who left out key elements from each type of conversation.

1. One manager had a quarterly meeting to announce the division's goals, but he did not connect them to the larger corporate goals or explain why the nonfinancial goals were as important as the financial ones. This is an Initiative Conversation without the *Why* element. This manager believed his employees' poor communication with other corporate offices was due to their lack of ability to link their work to the bigger picture, but he had not helped them make that connection.

2. Another manager explained a new procedure for submitting weekly status reports, but did not work with the staff to clarify the specifics about which communication channels and system authorizations were required. She had an Understanding Conversation without the *What* element. Those few staff members who knew about an available intranet reporting system did not have an opportunity to clarify the process for everyone else. When many employees failed to implement the procedure fully, this manager blamed them for not paying attention and resisting change, but if she had talked with them about her goals for the reporting process, they could have avoided the problem.

3. A supervisor asked an employee to undertake a project without stating the desired milestones or

the final deadline. He had a Performance Conversation without the The supervisor blamed the failure on the employee's incompetence and lack of commitment, but the fault was in the incomplete Performance Conversation.

4. An executive delegated a large responsibility to a senior staff person. He complimented the staff person on her ability to keep things organized and praised her as being the perfect person to do the job, but he dismissed her genuine resistance to accepting the new responsibility. The executive had a Closure Conversation without the

Michelle, a senior manager in Human Resources, is responsible for implementing a variety of programs in her organization, including the Training Project, which will eventually affect most of her organization's employees. Michelle reported that the Training Project was "not progressing well" despite the fact that she was, in her words, "talking about it all the time." Her team was missing deadlines and members' results were generally poor.

To determine why things were moving so slowly, Michelle reviewed her emails, memos, and meeting notes for the Training Project. Her review of past conversations confirmed that she was talking about the project often, and with the right people. It also suggested that the project launch had gone well, and that everyone understood the importance and intent of the Training Project, so she was confident that her Initiative and Understanding Conversations were not the problem.

"The Performance Conversations seemed okay too, " Michelle said, "because I made lots of requests. But then I noticed that I made most of those requests without mentioning the time by when things should be done. No deadlines! I might as well have been wishing instead of communicating! Second, I made very few promises, and I did not ask other people to make promises either. Third, I saw a pattern in the way I made requests: I continued to ask for the same things in the same way, without ever nudging people out of their comfort zones to do anything outstanding, beyond the ordinary. Finally, I saw that I was good at thanking people when they did things for me, but I was not following up with people who promised results but failed to deliver. I had no way to hold anyone accountable for what was not getting done. Bottom line: I never would have believed I was so sloppy in my communication with my staff. "

Michelle used Performance Conversations, but without including *When* she wanted actions and results, and without getting "good" promises. She realized she was never quite sure if people knew exactly what they were promising. She used Closure Conversations for appreciation, but she did not use them to follow through with people on *What* parts of their agreements were finished or to clarify what was still incomplete.

This meant she had no system to help people be accountable for their work or their promises.

By not using the four conversations completely, Michelle was unknowingly contributing to the failure of her team. Some of her conversations were actually slowing things down. When she began asking people to specify what they were going to do, adding timelines to her requests and promises, and following up on the status of requests and promises, the project's momentum picked up.

"We started having short weekly 'debrief' meetings, " Michelle said. "We reviewed what we had done and what was still on the list. We began seeing the victories instead of only the problems. Our meetings became little celebrations. People took on new tasks more happily than they did before. Within three weeks we were unstuck and back to making good progress on the Training Project."

Six Limitations to a Successful Workplace

Everyone wants to be successful at work. People want good performance reviews, raises, promotions, interesting job assignments, and a personal sense of satisfaction and accomplishment. Many people want to go beyond their personal success to include success for their teams or departments too. They want to meet organizational goals, have satisfied customers, enjoy good group morale, and work well with others. Personal and group successes contribute to a sense of self-worth, build confidence and competence, and make people feel good about their abilities and futures.

We have observed six workplace problems that limit these desired individual and group successes. Sometimes the problems are temporary but, in many instances, can become part of the culture of an organization. At their worst, they can compromise even the best employee talent and the strongest executive determination. In the face of certain persistent workplace problems, people either develop ways to get around them or become resigned to the futility of investing any further effort.

1. **Lateness.** In many workplaces, people regularly arrive late for meetings, finish jobs after their deadline dates, or don't respond in a timely manner to emails, phone calls, or memos, even the ones marked "urgent."

   Jeannette, an inventory control manager, says, "Our agency's finance team consistently sends us budget information, but on the finance team's schedule instead of ours. We need a lot of advance notice to purchase some items. When we cannot get the financial information to plan our purchasing, we miss other deadlines. Even when the team says it will be on time, it is not. This is a chronic problem for us."

Although lateness is frequently attributed to personal qualities, such as procrastination or laziness, it can become an organizational problem weakening communication between divisions, geographical regions, and hierarchical levels. Lateness, like many other performance problems, can be cured by altering our conversational patterns, especially by adding Performance and Closure Conversations (see Chapters 4 and 5). When managers make specific requests for on-time performance, and follow up on the group's overall timeliness, lateness declines across the board.

2.

Kate, an insurance account specialist, complains about poor quality, saying, "Our sales representatives give us bad data, or only part of the month's numbers instead of all of them. We go into the database and try to get the information we need ourselves, but sometimes we do not know where to look. We end up doing two jobs—theirs and ours. It's very frustrating."

Problems in quality may be due to a lack of talent, incentives, or attention to detail, and, over time, they can undermine the work ethic of all employees. It is possible to improve quality by improving the use of all four types of conversation on the part of managers and supervisors. Understanding Conversations in particular can restore awareness of goals and support alignment on how to measure and observe exactly what we mean by "quality" (see Chapter 3). Closure Conversations will support accountability and highlight the processes or materials that contribute to resolving quality breakdowns (see Chapter 5).

3.

John, a systems analyst, tells us, "Our decision support team leader is very unpleasant to work with. He is mostly nonresponsive and when he does respond, he blames us for the problems we are having. We ask him for things but he does not even make a note of it, so we know he is not going to remember or take action. My analysts are tired of hearing his criticisms about how we should have anticipated the problem and avoided it. So now we don't go to him as much as we should, even though he is smart and knows our technology better than anyone here."

When people are difficult to work with, we would prefer to stay out of their way rather than "deal with" them, but that choice turns one difficult person into everyone's problem. We can turn many difficult situations around if we are willing to modify our conversational pattern, especially by using more Closure Conversations to reduce the carryover of problems from the past (see Chapter 5) and refresh the Initiative Conversations to remind people of the new future we are working toward (see Chapter 2).

4. **Lack of Teamwork.** When people who are (or should be) working together toward the same goals begin to have trouble communicating or coordinating their work, we say they are lacking teamwork. In reality, team members may not share an understanding about the purpose of the team, the ways they need to communicate with other groups or internal customers, or the "best practices" they should be applying to their daily work.

Anna, a project manager for a new marketing campaign, claims, "We don't have any teamwork here ever since Tammy and Milt had a big argument in the conference room in front of everybody. Tammy has a group of seven people who have continued to do their job, but now they are doing it without Milt's input. Milt has printing expertise that Tammy's group does not have, but he will not meet with Tammy's group any more because he says the group was disrespectful to him. We have deadlines for quality and client service here, but everyone is paying attention to the personality feud instead of focusing on the work. It seems like the team is more about individual psychology than everybody working toward goals."

Personal agendas or unclear objectives and practices can undermine a team's synchrony, but we can restore teamwork by revitalizing the use of all four types of conversation. Initiative Conversations provide the context in which people are invited to put their personal interests in line with a new proposal (see Chapter 2). Understanding Conversations help people clarify their roles and adjust job responsibilities appropriately (see Chapter 3). Performance Conversations spell out the specifics of results and communication requirements to achieve the goals (see Chapter 4). Closure Conversations help support people in completing conflicts or disappointments from the past (see Chapter 5).

5. **Poor Planning and Workload Overwhelm.** Today, many people have more work to do than time in which to do it. New technologies, changing priorities, project scope creep, and "putting out fires" all contribute to a problem of overwhelm, a lack of planning, and ineffective scheduling habits.

   Andrew, who works in a small advertising company, says, "My boss is my biggest interruption. At least twice a week, she bursts into my office, panicked, carrying projects that would normally take days to complete and wants them done immediately. I cannot plan my work because everything could change in an instant and I am falling further and further behind on my promises to clients. I can't keep up with what I have and she keeps giving me more."

It is easy to believe that there is nothing we can do about an increasing workload or a manager or employee who is not planning properly. Yet, it is possible to gain more control over your workload by adjusting your conversational pattern, including better use of the Performance Conversation techniques for making complete and effective requests and promises (see Chapter 4).

6. **Insufficient Resources and Support.** One way to improve productivity is to tighten job constraints and specifications so that people need to become more creative and innovative to get their work done. But creativity and innovation will disappear if the tightening goes so far that people can't do their work properly.

Jackie, a customer service manager in a sales firm, reports, "The overall level of work has not changed, but our headcount has gone down so much that the work cannot be completed by the remaining people. I now have the work of three people, and our quality is beginning to suffer. Last week the company received seven customer email complaints, but we still cannot get the staff and telecommunications support we need to improve service. I don't know who to talk to about this, but if we don't take care of our customers, we'll all be out of business."

Many resource and support problems can be resolved by changing a conversational pattern. Performance Conversations are especially useful, as they encourage people to tie their requests for resources to promises for performance, thus opening a new dialogue for resource problems outside the usual "scarcity" model (see Chapter 4).

Although treated separately, these six limitations can reinforce and aggravate each other. Late or poor quality work, for example, undermines teamwork and increases the workload on others. Poor planning and insufficient resources result in late work, poor quality work, and workload overwhelm. Difficult people are often those who are late, do poor quality work, and undermine teamwork. The six limitations also contribute to distrust, lack of confidence, and ill will often found in poor working relationships, which in turn contribute to the occurrence of the six limitations. In Chapter 6, we will show you how several managers combined the four types of conversation to resolve the six limitations outlined above.

The good news is that we can reduce or eliminate the six limitations by updating our conversational patterns. Abraham did it, as did Michelle, Jason, and Tori. In each case, it requires knowing the four conversations to make things happen and improve productive relationships. It also requires being willing to consider that your own pattern of conversations could be a factor in holding the current situation in place.

Is it true that your talk is the cause of those limitations? Not necessarily, but it is a powerful point of view to take because it puts you in a position to introduce changes. If altering some of the conversational habits in your workplace can reduce or eliminate the effects of the six limitations, it will be worth the effort.

Conversations: Your Personal Advantage

As you learn and practice using Initiative, Understanding, Performance, and Closure Conversations, you will see new ways to address these six limitations and enhance communication, productivity, and relationships in your workplace.

Changing your conversational pattern is not difficult. It does not require extensive training or a change in your personality or values. All it takes is a willingness to examine your current conversational patterns, identify the types of conversations and conversational elements you are missing, and practice using them. This will expand and strengthen your conversational tool kit to support your success in a wide variety of situations.

In the following chapters, we explain the four types of productive conversations and the ways each one works. Examples from real managers and workplaces will demonstrate different aspects of each conversational type, so you can begin to practice using them right away. As with anything new, practicing each conversation in different settings, with different people at different levels and areas of your organization or community, will help you gain confidence and mastery in your communication. We promise a breakthrough in your success—and a personal advantage—with every additional conversation you master.

Key Points

1. Some conversations are not productive and take up people's time and energy without changing anything. Complaining, blaming, and gossip are usually not productive.

2. There are four types of productive conversations:

   a. Initiative Conversations get things started by proposing a new goal or future

   b. Understanding Conversations support input from, and discussion with, the people who will work toward the goal

   c. Performance Conversations are based on requests and agreements—ask and promise—to get specific about who will do what, and by when

   d. Closure Conversations are like erasing the past, and they focus on recognizing accomplishments and people, and clean up unfinished business

3. Each of your four conversations needs to include all six elements to be a complete conversation.

   a. Asking the questions *What-When-Why* will help you develop information about what you want to accomplish or make happen

   b. Asking the questions *Who-Where-How* will help you develop ideas about the resources and methods involved in making it happen

4. There are six workplace limitations—lateness, poor work quality, difficult people, lack of team-work, poor planning and workload overwhelm, and insufficient resources and support—that can be managed with the four types of conversations.

Chapter Two

Initiative Conversations: Create a Future

Landing a man on the moon began with an Initiative Conversation. On May 25, 1961, President John F. Kennedy went before a joint session of Congress and made the following proposal:

I believe that this nation should commit itself to achieving the goal, before this decade is out, of landing a man on the moon and returning him safely to the earth. No single space project in this period will be more impressive to mankind, or more important for the long-range exploration of space; and none will be so difficult or expensive to accomplish. Let it be clear—and this is a judgment which the Members of the Congress must finally make—let it be clear that I am asking the Congress and the country to accept a firm commitment to a new course of action, a course which will last for many years and carry very heavy costs. If we are to go only half way, or reduce our sights in the face of difficulty, in my judgment it would be better not to go at all.

What Kennedy proposed was, at the time, unimaginable. Scientists said they could not commit to a moon landing because the necessary knowledge and technology did not exist, and they were not sure they could invent it to meet Kennedy's timeline. The Russians had successfully orbited a man, Sr. Lt. Yuri Gagarin, around Earth, but Americans had accomplished only a suborbital flight, made by Alan Shepard. The "space race" had just begun, and America was already behind.

Eight years later, on July 20, 1969, the world watched in awe as Neil Armstrong took "one small step for man; one giant leap for mankind" away from *Apollo 11's* lunar excursion module (LEM) and onto the surface of the moon. With that step, and *Apollo 11's* subsequent safe return, America successfully accomplished the goal that Kennedy's Initiative Conversation had launched eight years earlier.

An Initiative Conversation is a proposal to create a new future, with the intention of making that future a reality. What makes an Initiative Conversation unique is not that it is a way of *talking about* starting something. It actually *does* start something. Not all Initiative Conversations end with a victory, as Kennedy's did. However, all victories do begin with an Initiative Conversation.

Leaders Have Initiative Conversations

Leaders point to a desirable future, and make it seem attractive enough and worthwhile so that we want to join with them in making that idea a reality. Are you in a position to propose a new project, make a change to your job or department, or contribute a suggestion to a committee or project team? If so, then you are in a position to lead by having an Initiative Conversation.

Most people believe that authority, titles, and positions of respect are not necessary in order to demonstrate leadership. Still, most people say they are not in a position to lead, because they do not think of themselves as leaders. Leadership is not restricted to the executive office, or to people at the top of the hierarchy. Leaders work at all levels of organizations, and people at all levels can be leaders.

A distinguishing characteristic of leaders is that they have Initiative Conversations. They envision a better future than the one we can predict given the way things are now. Leaders are willing to speak up, propose actions and outcomes, and encourage others to envision and participate in making a more desirable future into a reality.

A Future by Design

An Initiative Conversation is an active and intentional approach to the future. When we are passive, we drift through the passage of time and events. A twig, floating on the surface of a pond, carried by currents of water and wind, will be somewhere else in the future. In an hour, a day, or a week it may land on the shore across the pond, remain floating on the water, or sink to the bottom. The twig has no relationship to its future, drifting passively in the pond.

People are not twigs: we can create a future by design. We have desires or intentions, goals or plans, and can have an active relationship to the future. When we are passive, our future will be a product of the drift in our own environments, interactions, and habits. When we become active and intentional about our future, we can deliberately choose to make something happen. For example:

- A board of directors decides to sell off a product line to another company by the end of the year.
- A manager decides to reorganize her business unit to improve customer service before peak season.
- New parents decide to set aside savings for a child's college education.

The desire for something better is characteristic of human beings. To make your goals a reality, begin by having Initiative Conversations: announce the future you want to achieve, and invite other people to join you in making it happen.

- The board of directors announces the sell-off as part of its vision for a more streamlined and focused company.
- The manager invites a specialist to help her unit design a more efficient and effective structure for servicing customers.
- The new parents set up a college fund and invite family members to support reaching their savings goal.

Initiative Conversations are proposals that share an idea for an attractive and worthwhile future, and show people the possibility and the value of fulfilling it. An effective Initiative Conversation is more than simply a "good idea" or suggestion. It outlines the vision of reaching a goal or implementing a plan, says by when it can be accomplished, and adds a reason or value for doing it. This gives everyone a big-picture sense of what the future can be, when it is possible, and why it is desirable.

In many cases, the Initiative Conversation goes beyond informing people, and begins to engage them and excite them about being a part of making something happen. When an Initiative Conversation is effective, many people who grasp the vision and the opportunity will join in the process to create the new and desirable future.

Say What You Want + When and Why You Want It

Kate, the manager of Human Resources (HR), was dealing with an increasing number of internal complaints from her company's managers. The managers were impatient with lengthy delays in processing their new hires, promotions, and transfers. Kate was certain these complaints were due to a lack of technology tools and services needed by her staff. She blamed the Technology group for not supporting the HR office, and thus for indirectly not supporting all the managers in the company.

"I'm only an HR manager, so I don't have very much authority in this company, " Kate explained. "There is a bias here that favors the operations and technical personnel, and my vote doesn't always count as much as other managers' votes. In order to get a high-level manager to do something, I sometimes have to be more aggressive than I like to be. But in this case, I'm willing to do that because I'm tired of taking the blame for the long hiring delays."

Mitch, the director of the Information Technology and Systems (ITS) group, was reluctant to meet with Kate. He rightly suspected she would be critical of his department's services, but he had his own budget and personnel problems to deal with. He put off the appointment for more than a month, but at Kate's insistence, finally agreed to meet in a neutral conference room.

Kate started the meeting by putting three pages of statistics on the table that itemized the ITS team's response times over the past six months. The statistics showed that ITS technicians were taking longer and longer to respond to HR needs, and the number of complaints from HR personnel were rising.

Mitch began by defending his ITS technician, saying, "I agree, we should be more responsive, but my technicians are seriously understaffed and the backlog of jobs keeps growing. We are doing the best we can. I plan to hire new people in the next few months, and that should help, but I can't promise anything now." He went on to show genuine concern and expressed confidence that his department's performance would improve over time.

Kate said, "Yes, Mitch, they should do exactly what you say. But I want a solution now. You could implement a training program that would have them work more efficiently. You could focus on their performance and start tracking how many of their appointments actually resolve the technical problem they come to fix. Better yet, your technicians could start using the company's new Work Order Scheduling system to manage their work more accurately and promptly. Or maybe we should take these statistics to the operations manager and see what her solution is?"

Mitch picked up on Kate's reference to the operations manager, but continued his defense. "We don't have the budget for a training program, and it probably wouldn't help reduce our backlog anyway. We do track performance, but the technicians do not always agree with the customer about whether the problem is resolved or not, so we don't trust those numbers. And I think the company's Work Order Scheduling system is overkill for us, since we already have a good method of scheduling and tracking help requests."

"It's not good enough, Mitch, " Kate told him, stepping into a more assertive tone. "I want something new from you. Our HR group serves every employee in the organization. We work to meet state and federal requirements, satisfy union contracts, and help hire and train personnel to be better at their jobs. The past six months we have had poor technology service that slowed our own processing times, and most of the other managers are impatient with us. I would rather not have to tell them that you are the bottleneck. You and I need to talk about what will have your technicians provide timely support to everyone in the company, including my HR staff."

Kate was working hard to have an Initiative Conversation. The main ingredient of an Initiative Conversation is a statement of *What* you want and *When* and *Why* you want it. Kate made it clear she wanted better tech support and her approach to getting the idea across to Mitch used all three elements. She also stated the importance of her office's work for the company managers and other outside authorities and hinted at the consequences of failure. Kate implied that she might make the problems of ITS into a more public discussion, which could be uncomfortable for Mitch. She did not intend this to be a threat, but only to underscore how important it was to come to a new solution for the problem.

Kate made a proposal for new solutions and a compelling offer to work with Mitch on creating a plan for change. Mitch was going to have to do something new. This was an effective Initiative Conversation because Mitch got the idea, joined the Initiative Conversation, and agreed to work with her on creating a new short-term future.

Make It Positive

Mitch had been avoiding making changes in the ITS department. He was a new manager of the technicians, and he wanted to be successful in that position. He believed that happy employees would perform well, so he took special efforts to listen to their problems, improve their benefits and resources, and allow them to work in the ways they knew best. He avoided asking his people to learn new things or do more work, afraid of risking their disapproval and unhappiness. In particular, he wanted to avoid asking his technicians to switch to the new Work Order Scheduling (WOS) system. He had been complacent about the response time statistics, drifting along on his preference for pleasing, supporting, and not confronting people. Kate's direct approach made him very uneasy.

"I don't want to force a change on people, " Mitch said to Kate. "My technicians are specialists who solve difficult problems in a network environment with a complex mix of software and hardware needs. The last thing they need is someone telling them to change the way they work at the same time they are supposed to be improving their response time."

"But however brilliant they are, " Kate said, "they are not improving their response time." She pointed to the pages spread out on the conference table. "It's getting worse. Your technicians are the only people in this organization who are not using the WOS system, which means they are the only ones who have not changed the way they schedule appointments, close out their service orders, and report their results. They know how to install and service the WOS system for other departments, but they are not using it to manage their own work."

Mitch made one last objection, saying, "Every week in our staff meetings, the techs tell me about how many failures and glitches they see in supporting that WOS system. If I ask them to use the system themselves, I will look foolish, they will get hopelessly bogged down, and their back-logs will get worse."

"The WOS system works, " Kate said. "It's your techs who need to get on board. You are going to have to help them change, and help them develop their skills to do a better job for their customers. It is time you wanted them to be successful instead of comfortable."

"That's the moment, " Mitch said later, "when I realized I could get the technicians to use the new system, and that they wouldn't undermine service, get mad at me, or do anything disruptive. They were technicians, after all, and they would want to get it right. Until Kate pointed out that I was trying to avoid something negative—their resistance—I didn't see that I could try to cause something positive and help my technicians improve their success rate."

Most of us know more about what we do *not* want than about what we *do* want. People are quick to see what is wrong in any situation, what could or should be done about it, and who could or should fix it. Sometimes we pay more attention to our negative judgments than to our positive wants, and focus more on what we want to avoid than on what we want to accomplish. An Initiative Conversation must include something positive and attractive to invite people's attention.

Focus on the Goals, Not the Perils

Warren Bennis and Bert Nanus, in their book,

"Focus is the quintessential component of performance in every activity, " said Tim Gallwey, the bestselling author of *The Inner Game of Work.*[2] He claims we perform better when we focus on something specific and desirable that we want to accomplish, rather than on the dangers we want to avoid. Our attention pulls us toward its object: we will be more successful when we pay attention to what we desire than to what we dread. When we focus on our fears, we risk being pulled in the feared direction, but if we focus on what we want, the goal becomes our partner.

Mitch and Kate agreed that getting the technicians to use the WOS system was only a first step in improving tech support for all managers in the company. But they needed to keep their eye on that goal. They planned to meet once a week for half an hour to review the latest response time statistics and discuss actions to improve response performance. WOS software in his department, and Kate would provide HR training and support for the technicians as they went through the change. Both agreed not to get caught up in problems, but to stay on course to improving technology and HR support.

Choose Your Initiative Statement: What-When-Why

Once you have decided to initiate action toward a new future and planned your audience and message delivery, you need a summary statement of the initiative to serve as your basic announcement. Your "initiative statement" summarizes the

- *What* do we want to accomplish?
- *When* do we want it to happen?
- *Why* does it matter?

Focus on having the *What-When-Why* message reach everyone in your audience. This is not the time to give a lot of attention to "how" it will be done. Very often, as with the initiative to put a man on the moon, "how" to accomplish it is not fully known. As you move forward into using the other three types of conversations, you will be adding ideas and suggestions to continuously improve people's knowledge of "how" to reach the goal. Choosing your initiative statement gives you the way to communicate efficiently and attract people's attention to the *What-When-Why* of the future you are proposing.

What Do We Want to Accomplish?

What Do We Want to Accomplish?

President Kennedy's desired accomplishment was to "land a man on the moon and return him safely to the earth." This general outline was filled in over the next eight years with specifications of the types of fuels and metals to be developed and thousands of other specific achievements. Kennedy's audience understood that they would need to do a lot of work to flesh out the "how."

Kate and Mitch had a much smaller and more immediately available audience, some of whom they expected might object to their proposal or put up resistance. They chose to frame the new future as a joint venture to "deliver timely HR and technology results for all company managers and employees." Because they knew their primary audience, they added two more details, confident this would stimulate all the necessary dialogue to get the conversation started.

One addition, "staff promotions done in half the time, " would get all HR and ITS personnel interested in participating. As Kate said, "If it's about promotions, we've got their attention." The second, "100% use of the WOS system company-wide, " was a way of putting everyone on notice that the work scheduling system would no longer be optional for anyone in the organization.

Their *What* statement complete, Kate and Mitch put it on a poster that would hang in whatever conference room they scheduled for their joint meetings.

Table 1

Deliver timely HR and technology results for all company managers and employees:
- Staff promotions done in half the time
- 100% use of the WOS system companywide

The *What* element of an initiative statement needs to be brief and compelling enough to attract the intended audience into both the Initiative Conversation and all subsequent conversations for fulfilling the initiative. Some other examples include:

- "Eradicate extreme hunger and poverty, " the first of the eight UN Millennium Development Goals agreed to by all the world's countries and leading development institutions.

- "Our goal is to produce one gigawatt of renewable energy capacity that is cheaper than coal." Larry Page, *Google* co-founder, November 27, 2007.
- "China sets an air quality target for the city of Beijing of 238 'blue-sky' days in 2006, " Xinhua News Agency, January 14, 2006.
- "Our goal is to make a computer cost as little as $100 and distribute millions of them to the world's poorest children, " Nicholas Negroponte, quoted by David Kirkpatrick in *Fortune* magazine, September 28, 2005, *Fortune* magazine.

No one knows, at the time these goals are stated, whether they can or will be realized, or what barriers will have to be overcome. The initiative statement, however, leads people to consider what might be possible if and when the proposed new future is realized.

When Do We Want It to Happen?

Every goal needs a timeline—that is what makes the new future a specific event instead of an abstract idea. The UN Millennium Development Goals have a goal date of 2015. Larry Page set his timeline more loosely when he said, "It can be done in years, not decades." China promised the air quality goal for Beijing would be met in the year of the Beijing Olympics, 2008. The $100 laptop goal was originally set for 2008, but that goal was revised when the technology breakthroughs needed more time.

Some initiatives have a simple *When:*

- By this time next year, we will be in a new office building with a warehouse that allows us to have our entire inventory in one location.
- Within three months, we will have our environmental compliance policies drafted with policy implementation procedures in all of our production facilities.
- Starting today, we have a full-time person dedicated to updating our customer service Web site.

Kate and Mitch agreed to an overall six-month timeline that included time for the technology change plus time to capture data on the performance changes resulting from the initiative. Mitch set a two-week milestone to have his whole team using the WOS system. When he met with his vendors, he was able to develop a more specific plan for those two weeks. He scheduled the vendors to load the updated software, provide a half-day refresher training, and support two business process changes.

"The vendors told me that most of the software was already loaded, and the technicians didn't need much training, " Mitch said. "So I planned to focus on the business process changes. My techs had been using a work log to track their jobs, so the biggest change for them was to begin picking up their work orders from the new system instead of the manual log. It meant they needed to do some data entry and retrieval at the beginning and end of every day, and use mobile computing and dispatching throughout the day."

"The biggest problem, " he explained, "is that we won't be able to get the technicians their mobile computing capability ready in two weeks. It will take at least six weeks to get the right hardware to make them fully mobile. Until then, we'll keep using our beeper system, and the techs who are working in different offices around the campus will call in to our Central Command and get updated work order information."

Mitch was relieved that his techs were good sports about the change, and that his worst fears were not realized. He said, "They actually had fun inventing the Central Command idea and testing it out, so even the mistakes were not disasters. They joked about the 'learning opportunities' that they were having every day, and generally were much more upbeat than I expected. They were really enthusiastic about that two-week timeline."

Why Does it Matter?

The value of an initiative needs to be spelled out clearly for everyone, especially when it requires financial or material resources, or causes people inconvenience or extra work. The *Why* is a value statement that provides a context for the change and allows people to choose to spend their time, money, and effort to reach the goal. Leaders launching an initiative will already be enthusiastic about the new future, but they need to remember that their audiences may not recognize the value of the outcome and the difference it will make. Spelling out the impacts, benefits, and new opportunities will help people engage their best efforts to achieve the result.

One powerful way to communicate the value of an initiative is to tie it to your mission, vision, values, or strategies. Those things are usually stated in a positive way. Few people will be attracted to working on a timesaving or cost-cutting initiative, but many will be interested in positive-sounding purposes such as improved customer service, higher quality, or better communication between groups. When we invite people to work on something meaningful and positive that adds value to their organization or environment, they are more likely to be open to learning more about what is possible and how they might participate.

Mitch told Kate, "All that stuff you said about your HR department—about how you serve every employee and work with unions and state and federal laws—it made an impression on me. I have not given that kind of thought to what we do in ITS, but I would like to be able to talk about my department that way. I know it would be good for the techs."

Kate agreed, saying, "My HR staff is also happy with this new initiative. When staff members saw the poster of our goal, they told me this was the first time they ever saw the techs as their partners instead of their problem. We talked about how the company is growing, and how we need to move experienced people up so we can hire and train more staff. Our old system of spreadsheets, interview schedules, and signature processes was cumbersome, and nobody is sad to see it go. With your support on the new scheduling system, we have a good database that is easier for us to help the managers more quickly."

Prepare for Your Initiative Conversation:

Before taking your initiative on the road, consider

Who Needs to Participate?

Identify all the different individuals and groups you believe will be needed to accomplish the initiative. Who could do the work? Who could provide the resources? Who will receive the benefits? Who needs to authorize, approve, or regulate some aspect of the initiative? This is your first guess, which you will probably continue to revise as you go forward.

Kate said, "Once we were committed to taking action, we started planning who would play a part in our joint initiative. The first step was to see who would help implement this change or provide the resources to get it done. We made a list of all the important people in the company we needed to have on our team. At one point, we realized that each of us also had access to vendors who could support us in different ways, so we added them to our circle."

When in doubt about whether to include certain individuals or groups, it is usually best to err on the side of bringing them into the conversation. Bosses, for example, prefer to know about initiatives before they happen instead of being surprised when they are announced. The more people talking about an initiative, the more energy and attention it gets. When people feel included, they perceive the process to be fair, and are more willing to support it.

Where Will Resources Come From?

The process of taking an idea through an implementation process to its fulfillment requires resources. Before launching your initiative, consider what resources are likely to be required and where they might come from. Where could you get the money, the people, and the tools? Looking at an initiative's resource needs can be as simple as making a list of what you think will be needed to reach the objective.

We know one manager who always makes a "Likely Resource List" when he initiates a project or program. "Every resource has to come from somewhere, " he tells us. "I have found that sketching out what I think will be needed, and where I can get it, sets me up for more effective Initiative Conversations. In the process, I get a better sense of what I am proposing. Knowing where the resources might be gives people a starting point for considering the initiative."

Kate and Mitch said their resources were obvious. "They're the people, " they agreed. The technical people are resources who will learn to use the system. The technical vendors are a resource because they provide the tools. The HR people are a resource for learning supports—we have a good WOS training program and the technical staff will help us make it better as the staff members learn how to become WOS users and not just WOS fixers."

They identified other resources that would be necessary, including the WOS training sessions, mobile computing resources, and other communication supports. "Our list of resources, including where they will come from, is pretty simple, "Kate said. "We've done the WOS implementation before with other groups, so we can borrow from our previous plans."

As they progressed, they saw even more resources to obtain or confirm: staff time off for training, management support in the form of a directive that WOS would be a companywide mandate, and clerical support to keep track of work orders during the transition. Thinking about the resources and where they would come from helped them have more confidence in their initiative and its likelihood of success.

How Might the Work Get Done?

Even though you do not need a fully detailed work plan at the initiative stage, it is helpful to think through what might be involved in accomplishing what you are proposing. Are there steps or stages? Are there some complex jobs that should be broken into subtasks? Can some things be done simultaneously, while others must happen in sequence? Is there a schedule that might work, and are there some possible measures of success?

The objective is to begin sketching out what you think will be required to take you from idea to implementation to accomplishment. These are your initial thoughts and are meant to be suggestive rather than definitive. The prime benefit of doing this task now is that it lets you see where you need input and ideas from others and sets you up for Understanding Conversations.

Launch Your Initiative Conversation

At this point, you know *What* you want, *When* you want it, and *Why* it matters, and you have some ideas about *Who* is involved, *Where* the resources are, and *How* the work might be done. The next step is to have your Initiative Conversations and communicate to everyone the value of the future you want to build.

Some leaders launch initiatives by having one-on-one conversations, as Kate did with Mitch.

Others begin with a focus group to help add more definition to the future they want to create, or make a corporate or departmental announcement. Depending on the size and complexity of the initiative, you will want to design the way you "roll out" the message and launch the conversation.

Kate and Mitch came up with a variety of ways to support communication for the people involved in their project. They planned a way to introduce their initiative to the company's senior managers at the next management meeting. They agreed that they would put their "What" poster on the conference room wall for their weekly meetings, and they would take it to the management meeting too. They also set up times for the HR staff to meet with the ITS staff, and to be able to reach one another by phone and email.

They had Initiative Conversations with everyone on their list, and presented a proposal to the company's management team in a way that would gain support for the resource needs. They held a joint meeting of the HR staff and the ITS technicians to discuss details of the Work Order System initiative and to learn about their staff's ideas and concerns. They talked with their vendors to get the new software licenses and arrange delivery of several new pieces of equipment.

You can take your initiative out to people in many different ways: physical meetings, televised announcements, gala celebrations, telephone and video conferences, and pizza lunches are a few that we have seen. Using a variety of communication methods can be beneficial, because different people are comfortable with different communication media. Some people are happy getting an email announcement, while others want to be part of a discussion group or special event, and others want to be told personally.

The important thing is to include everyone who might have a direct or an indirect contribution to make to the fulfillment of the vision. You want to give people an opportunity to learn about the initiative and think about how their own activities and environment will change. Your goal for Initiative Conversations is to get people talking. Be prepared to give them your

There are many ways to open an Initiative Conversation. Some examples include:
- "I propose we start ... *What-When-Why*"
- "Beginning tomorrow, we will develop ... *What-When-Why*"
- "Our strategic objective is ... *What-When-Why*"
- "Today is the beginning of ... *What-When-Why*"
- "I want your support to implement ... *What-When-Why*"

You will probably say this same initiative statement many times. One important job for a leader is to keep the big-picture goals alive for people by repeating them as the initiative progresses toward completion. Initiative Conversations tend to have short lives. Even when things are going well, people get caught up in their local details, and the big picture fades from view, so they need frequent reminders about the purpose of their labors.

Using a poster, a map, or some other visual display can be a good way to keep the goals of your initiative alive for people. Mitch and Kate used the poster in their meeting rooms that summarized the initiative statement. The United Way puts a "thermometer" out where everyone—staff and donors—can see the goal and the status every day. NASA's Space Station offices had a sign in the hallway that read: "Number of days until launch is..." Someone updated the number every day. Some people working on the $100 laptop project have mock $100 bills stuck to the walls throughout the project area. These displays are quick and clear reminders of the future that people are working to realize.

You do not need to be certain of success in order to invent a possibility and invite others to participate in fulfilling it. In fact, if success were certain, the desired outcome would not require any special creation or engagement. A little risk, or an uncertain outcome, can be excellent seasoning to spice up an initiative. The U.N. Millennium Development Goals are inviting, at least in part, because they are ambitious, complex, and uncertain.

The Leader's Intent

The U.S. Army has a doctrine known as the commander's intent. According to its Field Manual, the commander's intent:

- Describes the desired end state—it is not a summary of the whole operation, but will serve as the single unifying focus for all levels of subordinates
- Is a clear and concise statement of the purpose of the operation, because long narrative descriptions "tend to inhibit the initiative of the subordinates"
- Must be understood two levels below the level of the issuing commander—its purpose is to focus subordinates on what has to be accomplished in order to achieve success, and to discipline their efforts toward that end[3]

Leaders and managers can take a lesson from the commander's intent. The idea is to focus everyone's attention on "end states" (i.e., where we want to be, not on which pitfalls to avoid). Organizations, like battlefields, are volatile, uncertain, complex, and ambiguous (though hopefully not lethal). Leaders, including commanders, cannot guarantee control of a project merely through their personal presence. By specifying objectives as clearly and concisely as possible, subordinates are more able to take self-generated action to move everyone toward the objective.

Whether you are a CEO, a department manager, or a team member, as a leader your intent is to engage people in collaborating to turn a possible and beneficial future into a reality. Your success will be a product of your own enthusiasm and commitment to that future, and your ability to regenerate the initiative often enough to keep others enthusiastic too.

If You Are Missing Initiative Conversations

Initiative Conversations are available to anyone with an idea for making a beneficial change—you can use them in your workplace, your home, or anywhere. There are many people, however, who do not know that this kind of conversation is available, or how to use it properly. Sometimes people get so accustomed to certain speech habits that they do not see how or where to use Initiative Conversations, or how to use them more effectively.

If You Don't Use Initiative Conversations

When there is something you want to accomplish, you cannot afford to leave out Initiative Conversations. It takes some thinking, and probably some collaboration, to spell out

When you share the initiative with all the people who will be part of making it real, you are telling them, "Let's do *What-When-Why*." This is a powerful way of calling people to consider creating a new future. It establishes a context of value *(Why)*and the specifics that make it possible to envision the actions and outcomes to accomplish it *(What-When).* Leaders who pass over the Initiative Conversations are missing the chance to set a strong foundation for engaging people. Start your desired accomplishment off well with a statement of *What-When-Why,* and use it often throughout the implementation phase.

Not everyone wants to make new things happen. Some people are happy with the status quo, but they are not usually successful as managers and leaders. For the most part, people want improvements, even though they sometimes complain about too much change. In an organization where everything stays the same, and there are no new goals or initiatives, people become complacent. When you add in a few Initiative Conversations, you liven things up and get people moving. The energy can even reach beyond your vision to light up other projects and get people thinking about making improvements in a variety of ways and places you never imagined.

If You Use Them Improperly

The most important rule of Initiative Conversations, as with all four types of conversation, is to use all six elements. If you are unclear about the

There are other ways Initiative Conversations can be used improperly. One example is the story of a little boy who went into the school principal's office and found nobody there. He spotted the microphone for the school's public address system, and switched it on. "School is over for the day, " the little boy said into the microphone. "Everybody should go home now."

Excellent initiative, but he lacked the authority to make that call. You may be positioned to announce

a corporate merger or make the decision to purchase a new car, but if you are not, using a well-
developed Initiative Conversation will not help you
succeed in those areas without a strategy for engaging the decision makers. Some initiatives require key players to get them launched in a way
that they will be successful. But most of us can
initiate at least some improvements in our work
and home lives, and many people can launch
sizeable initiatives if they choose to do so.

Another improper use of Initiative Conversations is trying to accomplish something when you
do not have the ability to sustain the resource
commitments required for its completion. A manager with an unpredictable budget, for example,
may not be able to commit to a long-term hiring
and training plan. Some goals are too big to take
on all at once. Breaking big ideas into smaller
implementable ones can demonstrate the possibilities of a new future without breaking the bank or
creating discouragement in the workforce.

If You Use Too Many Initiative Conversations

Some people specialize in initiating things.
These are the good-idea people, and every workplace should have some of them. But in high-level
management positions, these people can get so
many things going that they cannot follow through

on them all, and some initiatives die for lack of attention. A manager who comes up with lots of new ideas for improvements and changes might get people excited at first, but without using the other three types of conversation to sustain the initiative, people lose interest. After the fiftieth great idea of the month, people will roll their eyes when the fifty-first is proposed.

Too many initiatives can lead people to question the credibility of the initiator, lose confidence in the initiative, and disengage from their own work. When people are not sure about what is serious work and what it just hot air, they tend to ignore all new ideas and withdraw, concentrating on what is immediately in front of them. Use your Initiative Conversations to launch the work you are committed to seeing come to fruition.

Putting It into Practice

Initiative Conversations create a vision for people to make a new and better future for themselves and others. We call the people who use Initiative Conversations "leaders, " because they are interested in creating new, positive futures and engaging all the right people in making things happen. Being a leader is not reserved for only the few—everyone can use Initiative Conversations to reach their goals at work and in other areas of life.

You can start by making a list of a few of your most valued goals. What do you want for yourself and others in the next three, six, or eighteen months? Saying what you want can be difficult, because it requires you to suspend your relationship with all the realities of today and envision something that does not exist yet. But surely there are things you want to make happen, wish to implement, or desire to change into something better—these are goals that you want to accomplish, not things you hope will fall from the sky. See if you can pry yourself loose from today long enough to fill in something like the table below:

List of Initiatives

What do I want to accomplish? (State the end result or outcome)	When do I want to accomplish it? (Be as specific as you can)	Why do I think it is important? (State the difference that you believe it will it make)
1		
2		
3		

Table 2

You now have an Initiative Statement for some of the outcomes that matter to you. For each initiative, there will be people who can help you to accomplish it, resources required, and some ideas on how it can be done. Start building the list for each outcome you want, as suggested in the table below:

For each Initiative

Who needs to participate? (List all individuals and teams)	Where will resources come from?	How might the work get done?
1		
2		
3		

Table3

Practice is simply a matter of having the Initiative Conversations with the people you have identified. Try telling people

Chapter Three

Understanding Conversations: Include and Engage

You already know what happens when you take a good idea or an initiative out to people: they will talk back. They will offer their good ideas and suggestions, maybe adding a few complaints and attitudes. They may even resist some of what you say.

The reason for most "resistance" (sometimes known as avoiding a new idea) is that most people are humming along in their lives, doing just fine without your proposal to try something new. In fact, your initiative risks making some people change what they are doing, perhaps moving them into unknown territory, which they may not wish to do. An initiative can present the classic threat of adult learning: that I will have to learn something new, I will have to do it in front of other people, and I might make a mistake and embarrass myself. Nobody wants to look foolish before his or her peers.

To avoid the trap of getting tangled up in dealing with resistance, it is important to remember two things. First, people

People want to fit in, belong, and be engaged in their surroundings. That is why you want to design and conduct your Understanding Conversations to help people find a way to participate in working toward the desired outcome. It is always a mistake to assume people know what to do, or how to do it: we do have to tell them what we want. But it is equally a mistake to only *tell* them what to do and how to do it. The challenge is to conduct a conversation that lets people create their own entry into the new proposal and to find a way to engage their interests and abilities while reducing their fears.

Understanding Conversations are a vital process for engaging people in owning and coauthoring a plan of action. When you provide people an opportunity to talk about the future and discuss how it will affect their daily activities and communications, you also gain the opportunity to improve your plan to reach a goal. All the input from Understanding Conversations is useful in developing a plan of action that benefits from the expertise of everyone involved.

Help People Find a Positive Meaning in Your Message

People are meaning-makers. Whatever happens, we can be counted on to understand what it means, and if we don't understand it, we will work hard to figure out the meaning. Sometimes we accept the meaning that others give to us, and sometimes we make up meanings without talking to anyone or testing our interpretation against reality in any way.

Jenine, a corporate change agent, did an informal survey of reactions to corporate announcements. She told us, "When our CEO announced that our marketing division was going to relocate to the Poughkeepsie office, he stated clearly that the purpose of the move was to have marketing work more closely with the consumer research division. But I was amazed at what people 'heard' in this announcement. Here are some of the things people said about what the CEO's announcement 'really meant'":

- A product-manufacturing executive said, "The CEO is going to change our product lines based on consumer research, which is going to change our equipment configuration, which will hammer the engineering and maintenance budgets for years to come. I've got a big job ahead just to control costs."

- A sales manager said, "They are going to come up with a new sales campaign, and making the change will cut our commissions in half. It's all because marketing didn't get its job done. I'm going to have to plan for a lot more travel expenses next quarter so my sales reps can reach way more new sales contacts."

- A computer network coordinator said, "This is the beginning of closing this entire office and moving our headquarters to Poughkeepsie. My wife and I just bought a home here, and I don't want to relocate, so I am going to start looking for a new position somewhere else in this area."

"In every case, " Jenine said, "people heard the CEO's message through their own thinking and perceptions, associated with the particular group they worked in. Whether in accounting, sales, or operations, every group has its own way of talking and understanding the larger world around it. This is true of individuals too. When someone has just bought a house, had a new baby, or gotten a medical diagnosis, everything the person hears will be related to that. People look to see how one change will alter the many ways they have their lives arranged."

When you introduce a new idea, or a plan to change anything, people will have questions about how it relates to them and how they will have to alter their habits and activities. The bottom-line question they are really asking is, "What does this mean for me?" Some of the ways people look for meaning when confronted with a change of any kind are by asking:

- How does this change my current position?
- Will I have to work with new people?
- How am I going to do these new tasks or talk to those new people?
- Why should I care about this? Can I just stay out of it?

We can never assume that the *What-When-Why* of our initiative statement will survive translation into everyone's unique world of thought and perception. The purpose of having Understanding Conversations is to give people the opportunity to interact with the initiative and gain a positive meaning for their own roles in creating the future. This does not mean they will be fearless or free of concerns, but perhaps they can see a way to participate and contribute, and to know that they can always ask questions and reshape their roles as needed.

The Setup: Repeat the Initiative and Add a Customized Who-Where-How

We can help people understand a goal or change by setting up opportunities for them to ask and answer questions about the proposed initiative. Depending on the size or complexity of the initiative, it may be necessary to do some serious planning and preparation to engage people. This is the time to bring out all six of the traditional journalism questions: the

Darryl, the director of the electricity department in a Midwestern city, illustrated what may be the most efficient Understanding Conversation we have ever seen. His department is responsible, among other things, for maintaining the city's streetlights as well as providing electricity to developers who build new residential or commercial developments within city boundaries. Darryl's department competes with the local electric company to service the builders, so he wants to deliver quality service at a competitive price. The electricity department's revenue contributes to the city's operating budget, which is an important part of the mayor's plan to avoid tax increases.

During the past few months, Darryl received several complaints from building developers that the electricity department's work was both late and of poor quality. One builder complained that area lights in the parking lot at his Eastside Shopping Center were installed a week late and only half of them worked. The problems delayed the opening of his shopping center and triggered an embarrassing media report.

Although Darryl had successfully dealt with similar situations in the past, this builder was politically well connected and made his dissatisfaction known directly to the mayor's office. "I got a phone call from the mayor's office that made it very clear I needed to fix the problem, and I needed to do it yesterday, " Darryl reported. "I can't afford to have any more complaints like this in the future."

Darryl called his two senior managers into his office: Alex, the manager of engineering, and Tony, the manager of installation. "Gentlemen, we have a serious problem, " Darryl said. "I just got off the phone with the mayor and he is unhappy. He got a complaint from the Eastside developer about our failure to get the lights installed on time and working properly. I'm asking you both to do whatever you have to do to fix it immediately, and when it's done I want to see you both back here in my office."

That was all Darryl needed to say. His communication to Alex and Tony reminded them of the original Initiative Conversation, stating the goal in terms of *What-When-Why:* he wanted the developer to be satisfied with area lights at the Eastside Shopping Center, the job to be done now, and to be aware that the mayor is watching. He was able to be very brief and to the point in this conversation because of the long experience he shared with his managers in their years of work for the city. In just a few sentences, he gave them his message, "Drop everything else and make this problem go away as soon as possible."

Alex and Tony had no further questions, nodded their heads, and returned to their own offices. Alex had worked with the builder in the engineering design phase of the project, and called him right away to discuss how to resolve the problem. Tony already had an installation crew working onsite at the Eastside parking lot, and called to confirm that the job was almost complete. When the crew captain called him back to say that everything was finally working, Tony called Alex. "I guess we'd better head on in to Darryl's office, " he said.

Most Understanding Conversations are not this efficient. Still, Darryl followed all the rules. He reminded them of the initiative—a successful Eastside development project—and he answered the three questions that set up an Understanding Conversation:

If Alex and Tony had needed more information, Darryl would have interacted with them to be sure they understood everything. But years of solving similar problems made this conversation easy and fast. In fact, Darryl told us later that he probably could have completed the entire Understanding Conversation in only three words: "mayor, unhappy, Eastside."

Help People Fit Into a Proposed Change

Rodd Wagner and James Harter report on a Gallup poll in their book *12: The Elements of Great Managing.* It showed that employees behave differently when they know how their job fits into the grand scheme of things.[1] When people agree that "The mission or purpose of my company makes me feel my job is important, " their organization has better profitability, fewer accidents, and lower turnover.[2] People who know *Why* they are working say that their work seems less like a forced assignment and more like something they have chosen to do. That is why reminding them of the *Why* in the initiative statement is important. Having Understanding Conversations about the proposed changes in work and resources will help to engage them even further.

The goal of Understanding Conversations is to have people discover for themselves what role they can play in accomplishing something. A leader or manager can tell someone, "This is your role in the new project, " but each individual needs to understand the change in his or her own terms and frames of reference. For example:

- Will this change present a challenge to my current position or abilities?
- Is this an opportunity for advancement?
- Is it a chance to use my skills and talents?
- What is the likelihood of success or failure?
- How can I increase my chances of success?

Understanding Conversations are ultimately very personal as people evaluate their own situations in light of the new initiative. The changes could raise someone's concerns about his or her communication skills or other abilities, the activities he or she will have to perform, and the implications for career goals. The idea is to have people interact and create a relationship between their existing way of working and the new proposal for a new future.

Be sure to tell people which facts of the proposal have already been decided and which are open to revision. If nothing is open to revision, of course, you will have to own up to the fact that you are either giving them an announcement or taking a survey, neither of which is an Understanding Conversation.

New Vocabulary: A Valuable By-product

One valuable by-product of asking and answering questions about an initiative is the new language that arises in the process. Even simple words and phrases can have vastly different meanings for people in different groups or departments.

One executive gave an example of the development of new vocabulary, saying, "I proposed an initiative to my management team when I told the team that I wanted to improve communication between our sales office and our service teams. I said the purpose of the initiative was to be sure that our deliveries to customers would never, never be late. I told them my plan to get the new process in place within two months, and our success measure was to have our customer service ratings break 95% excellent this quarter."

"I was not prepared for their response, " he said. "We had an argument for the rest of the meeting about the term 'late.' The sales people had one definition, the service teams had their own ideas about lateness, and the call center had a third and completely different idea."

This manager's Understanding Conversation came down to a lengthy and complicated discussion about the meaning of one word. Everyone had to sort out how his or her own job would change depending on which definition of "late" would be adopted. The sales people were accustomed to a due date that was agreed to only with the customer. They never checked with the service teams first to confirm whether they could accomplish the delivery by that date. This left the service people in a constant hurry to meet promises in which they had no vote.

The eventual resolution was that the sales and service people would agree on the date before confirming it with the customer. A simple solution, but it added an extra step to the sales people's job: talk to service before committing to the customer. The new definition of "late" was when a job did not meet the date agreed by all three: customer, sales, and service.

People assume that words are self-explanatory and meanings are universal, but reasonable people have different points of view, speak different languages, and create different meanings for everything that happens. An accountant and a quality control specialist, for example, use words like value, training, or effectiveness in very different ways. Many corporations have learned that when they launch a "quality improvement" initiative, they will soon be discussing the various definitions of "quality." Understanding Conversations help set a foundation to allow people from different backgrounds to communicate about a proposed course of action and align on a vocabulary that will support achieving the future outcomes.

Some managers find it enormously frustrating to deal with the personal views of individual workers, or hash out what people mean by a single word or phrase. However, research tells us that people have a greater sense of responsibility, and psychological ownership, for those parts of their life and work where they have a say in the matter.[3] Even when their own preferences do not ultimately win out, their willingness to engage in work deepens when they have gotten their views into the conversation.

Expand and Deepen Participation

It is safe to assume that most people are already busy and their calendars are as full as they want them to be. Proposing anything new is like topping off a gas tank: in very short order, the tank will be full and everything you are trying to add will spill out over the top. Whenever you want to initiate something, you are asking people to change the roles and goals they have created for their work, family, or finances, even if only in a small way.

Not all Understanding Conversations are as quick and clean as the ones in Darryl's electricity project. In a complex organization, or to implement a major change initiative, a manager must make special arrangements to engage people in the conversation. When you are ready to engage people in an Understanding Conversation, you will want to be ready to benefit from all of the

It is useful to make a plan or checklist for talking with people: what points to cover, what kinds of questions to answer, and how much information is known or available or needed. An Initiative Conversation rocks the boat, but an Understanding Conversation can help people find their place in the boat and grab an oar to move things forward. The goal of this conversation is to engage people in thinking about what the initiative means for them, and how they can contribute to the implementation of new plans and ideas for its accomplishment.

Host Question-and-Answer Sessions

All of the people who are necessary to accomplish an initiative are already conducting their lives with some kind of order and purpose. If you want to make something new happen, you must engage their attention, interest, and commitment. One way to do this is to schedule question-and-answer (Q&A) sessions to discuss the initiative in more detail. This helps people make sense of impending changes, and consider how to adapt their daily activities and interests to the proposal at hand, by asking their own questions and listening to other people's questions and ideas.

Some managers want to "shoot first and ask questions later," believing that time spent in meetings to talk about individual concerns is time wasted. But having insufficient Understanding Conversations can end up creating more work, not less. Furthermore, your investment in understanding can have a big payoff in productivity and teamwork.

Cathy was the CEO of Auto Town, a network of auto rental, repair, and refurbishing franchises, and her company faced stiff regional competition. She wanted to implement a strategic plan to make substantial changes to Auto Town's organizational structure, compensation system, and vendor network. She and her senior managers planned a series of "town hall" Q&A meetings, one in each of the eight locations of the company's operations, to discuss the plan with employees at all levels.

A month before each Q&A event, the managers distributed copies of the new strategic plan to every location, and began talking about it in their weekly staff meetings. The plan was available for anyone to read, but news about the changes traveled fastest along the grapevine of social conversations in each region. Within two weeks, employees at every franchise were well acquainted with the proposal for the Auto Town change initiative.

Ten days before each Q&A, the CEO asked her communication team to give all employees at the scheduled location a two-sided card to fill out. On one side was the question, "What do you want the Auto Town management team to know about you, your work, and your workplace?" On the other side, the question was, "What do you want to know from the Auto Town management team?" The communication staff asked everyone to fill out their answers and drop them into a collection bin by the end of the week.

When cards were collected from each respondent, the communication staff drew up a summary of all the responses for the group, and organized them into topics for the management team to review. Then the communication staff called a meeting of the whole Auto Town management team to show the managers what to expect from the upcoming Q&A. This gave the managers a greater understanding of the issues and concerns of employees, including their reactions to the new strategic plan and the organizational changes. The managers prepared their presentation prior to the Q&A in a way that they could address the specific questions and concerns of the employees at each location.

"We learned that there were a lot of job security worries, " one manager said. "Even though we already told people we were not going to downsize. The meeting preparation let us see that we needed to emphasize some things and allow more time for interaction on certain topics."

Cathy, the CEO, said, "We know we helped the mid-level managers and supervisors by taking the company's strategic plan to everyone. The communication cards helped us learn to speak the language of the different workplace environments. As a result, our employees knew we heard them, and many of them have now chosen to participate in some of our new strategy implementation teams."

The interactions in a Q&A Understanding Conversation will be a product of the assumptions participants have about what is expected of them. Cathy told her communication staff to make sure everyone knew she truly wanted to hear their perspectives and concerns. That message, plus the open questions on the comment cards before the meetings, set the tone for an open dialogue. The data from the cards gave the management team a greater understanding of the issues and opportunities at all locations and all levels of staff, and gave the managers time to consider their responses.

A university classroom is another example of a Q&A session. Many of Jeffrey's MBA classes had low student participation until he discovered why his students were not speaking up in response to his questions. He had wondered if they were lazy, unprepared for class, or just did not know the material, and complained to a colleague. "The students in this class don't seem very smart, or don't care much about learning." He even wondered if the university was admitting lower qualified students or if the nonparticipation was characteristic of the newest generation of graduate students.

When Jeffrey told his students that their lack of participation would hurt their class evaluations, one student spoke up and said, "You say you want participation, but your questions seem like a trap because we don't know how to give you the right answers." This led to a class discussion, revealing that students believed there was a "right" answer to every question a professor asked. One of Jeffrey's favorite questions was, "What did you learn from implementing the assignment in your workplace?" Students thought he had a list of certain lessons they should have learned, so they were not confident about what to say. Even though Jeffrey thought he was asking open questions, the students believed that attempting to answer was taking a risk.

Jeffrey realized he had to change his style of asking questions to reassure people that he was genuinely interested to hear what they had learned. He said, "There is no right answer to this question. I am interested to hear your observations about this assignment, and how it played out when you applied it to your job." The students began raising their hands to contribute their observations, and participation increased.

Remind People of the Initiative's Value and Consequences

Communicating the value of success and the consequences for failure is one effective way to have people understand how an initiative relates to them. This approach works best when the group understands that both "success" and "failure" relate to the initiative, and not to the individuals involved. People are sensitive to hints of individual rewards or punishment. They want to understand the relationship between their own personal success and the success of the initiative. It takes attention to be sure you define success for the initiative first, and separate it from any individual performance assessments.

Darryl in the electricity department was an example of using a "value and consequences" approach to engaging people. He only needed to tell Alex and Tony that the mayor was unhappy. That one fact summarized the rewards and consequences for solving the customer's problem. All three men knew a happy mayor can recognize and reward good results, and an unhappy mayor could make life difficult for city employees. Neither Alex nor Tony felt threatened, but they understood the importance of the situation and were willing to work to get favorable attention—and avoid unfavorable attention –from City Hall.

In another example, Cathy, the Auto Town CEO, said, "I let everyone know that we were in a major competitive situation, and that implementing our new organizational and marketing strategies was critically important. All our managers knew we needed everyone on board with these changes. The consequences of failure were unthinkable, but we were confident we could engage people in seeing the challenges the company was facing, not just the challenges of their particular job. We believed that if everyone understood, people would be stronger partners with us. Now that the strategy teams are producing good results, I believe we have been proven right."

The example of the MBA students also points to the use of "value and consequences." Students already have a grading system that clarifies the rewards and consequences of doing well in their coursework. But when Jeffrey reminded his students that their lack of participation would hurt their evaluations, it encouraged them to speak up about their concerns. The resulting conversation opened up a new level of participation in classroom discussions.

Reminding people of the rewards and consequences associated with an initiative helps them see why they should engage in the Q&A discussion. When we reduce or remove the perceived threats to communication, people can listen more openly without protecting themselves or ignoring the initiative. The conversation can then accomplish its goal of assisting people to consider their own participation in a new initiative.

Give People Problems and Ask for Solutions

In the electricity department, when Tony's crew had completed installing and testing all the shopping center lights, he went back to Darryl's office, where Alex was already describing his conversation with the developer. The three men were glad to hear the developer was now satisfied and that he was even going to call the mayor to let him know his problem was solved.

"Okay, this particular emergency is over, " Darryl told Alex and Tony. "But I don't like the idea that the mayor is personally watching to see whether we're doing our jobs. The Eastside lights aren't the only problem we've had lately. I've gotten several complaints about installation delays in the last few months, and each problem seems to involve both of you guys. There is something going on between engineering and installation, and I want you to find out why you have had more late installments than usual. Just give me the reason for the installation delays and tell me what will solve it. And see if you can do it in one week, will you?"

Alex and Tony knew three recent installations had been late, and in one case, a portion of the lights had not worked as planned. Privately, each manager blamed the other. Alex told us, "The installation crews aren't following our engineering plans. They go out and do what they think is right instead of following the plans."

Tony was equally self-justified, saying, "The engineers send us bad information. Sometimes they leave out key facts like where the trunk line is, or what voltage we can run with the transformers on the site. They want us to load up the lines, but we are not going to do that. My guys trust their own experience more than engineering's paperwork."

Darryl's demand to find the solution gave Alex and Tony a mandate to work together. It also gave them a riddle to solve, which served the purpose of answering the *Who-Where-How* question for them. "It's like he told us to be detectives, "Alex said, "and to scour the whole department to find out the answer. We have to find out *Who* is doing the work, *Where* the resources and deliverables are, and *How* the work gets done by looking at the whole department, not just our own people."

Tony agreed, saying, "We can even go outside the department if we need to. He wants an answer, and he is counting on us to find it. So what's the plan?"

"Instead of saying we know the solution, how about if each of us goes to talk to our people about this, "Alex proposed. "They might get interested in solving the puzzle. Let's ask them why those three jobs were late and see what they say. They'll tell us who else we need to talk to."

"Good, "Tony agreed. "Then let's get *them*to write down all the problems they encountered on those three jobs, instead of us doing it. And they should tell us which ones caused the biggest time delays, plus their ideas on solutions, too."

This set up the Understanding Conversation across a large number of people in four different groups in the electricity department: engineering, installation, inventory, and computer operations. Asking people to find solutions can be an effective way to engage them in a conversation, especially when they are sure they are not at risk of being held responsible for the problem. They put a few "setup questions" out into the workforce, and everyone who engaged in the conversation took a closer look at the processes for planning and implementing electricity jobs for developers. Alex and Tony said it stirred up conversations that made people more aware of the details of their jobs and the importance of communication.

Develop a Schedule and Performance Measures

The collaboration between Kate and Mitch to improve communications between the human resources (HR) office and the information technology service (ITS) groups was going so well that they didn't think they needed to do anything but "roll out the plan, " as Kate put it. They had a good statement of the initiative: improve HR processing times and ITS response times. Further, they believed every goal needs a timeline, so they moved ahead to create a schedule for implementing the changes and turned it into a second poster for the conference room.

"Showing people a visual display of the timeline will let every person in each group understand the deadlines that relate to their part of the project, " Mitch said.

"What about performance?" Kate asked. "How will they know when we are making progress?"

"We have the schedule of the deadlines, " Mitch said. "We can make up a scoreboard too, so that they can see what we want to have happen." After some discussion, they made up two measures for HR success, and two for ITS:

- HR—number of days to complete the new personnel hiring process
- HR—number of days to complete internal promotions and transfers
- ITS—percentage of technical service requests processed in the work schedule system
- ITS—percentage of technical service requests satisfied within one, four, eight, and twenty-four hours

Ready to tell everyone else what they had created, Kate and Mitch scheduled an "action assignment meeting" for Thursday morning. They posted both the schedule and the scoreboard on the conference room wall next to their initiative statement poster, and then sent an email out to notify all their staff members about the meeting in the morning. One sentence in the memo said, "We will review the timeline and the performance measures for the new HR-ITS collaboration project."

Within an hour of the email, a small crowd had assembled in the conference room to look at the two new posters. People began buzzing with questions about them:

"Are these measures for work days or calendar days?"

"Does the clock start when the work request is sent to ITS, or when an ITS staff person turns it into a work order?"

"Who will track the measures?"

"How often will they be reported?"

"Who will see the results? Do they go to upper management?"

Kate and Mitch arrived early for their meeting on Thursday, unaware that people had taken a sneak peek at the posters. They were ready to talk about assignments for who would track measures, prepare reports, update the schedule, etc., and were surprised to see many of their people already there. They quickly sensed the tension in the room, and it did not take long for the questions to tumble out. People seemed angry they had not been included in creating the time-line and the performance measures. After only a few minutes, Kate waved the discussion to a halt.

"Stop, " she said. "This schedule is not cast in concrete. We can change it. We just wanted to put a sample up in front of you so we could discuss it. The same thing with the performance measures: these are not the perfect measures. They are just something to get us started talking about how we can tell if we are making progress toward our goals."

"Absolutely, " Mitch said. "And all those questions you asked? We don't have the answers. We need you to help us come up with the answers. Should we measure work days or calendar days? We don't know. Who should see the results? We need your input to help finalize that kind of thing."

Kate and Mitch had not planned for a Q&A session, believing they could move directly from the statement of the initiative into handing out action assignments. The participants turned the meeting into the Q&A session they needed, and got talking about the measures and the timeline. Everyone settled down as Kate and Mitch allowed time to ask questions and collaborate on finding good answers.

"We dodged a bullet, " Mitch said later. "We didn't realize they would want to talk so much about the schedule and the measures. It was good, though, because they really got into it and came up with some details and changes that we never thought about."

In the process of discussing project infrastructures like the schedule and the performance measures, people began to see how their jobs might change, and whom they would have to work with in the other group. They generated ideas about how to satisfy the timeline while improving their group's performance on the measures. The Q&A Understanding Conversation gave them a new sense of *Who-Where-How* they would act and communicate in their changing work environment, and made improvements in the schedule and metrics.

One outcome of effective Understanding Conversations is to have a more developed timeline for the work to be done and the resources to be available.

Schedules with milestones, dates when different groups need to interact, and deadlines for results and deliverables can be created most effectively when they are done in Understanding Conversations. The group creates a momentum of finding a workable timeline, and each representative can contribute their perspective on constraints and opportunities that no single individual can provide.

Schedules and measures are useful tools to promote Understanding Conversations because they are so provocative. Most people use a calendar, and everyone cares about his or her own performance, so they are able to talk about those things. Because they can be so provocative, however, it is wise to take a tip from Kate and Mitch: Make sure everyone knows that the proposed schedule and any measures you bring into the meeting are in pencil, not in ink. Let them know that these things are just a draft example intended to get them thinking and talking. Then be diligent about incorporating the revisions they recommend so they know you mean what you say. People need their input considered to become part of shaping the proposal.

Engage the Next Circle of People

Sometimes all the employees do not fit into one room, or even a series of Q&A sessions. In the electricity example, four groups had input on the department's performance problems: engineering, inventory, installation, and computer operations. Instead of calling a meeting, the managers asked each group to give their comments on the recent problems with electricity jobs. The results showed four different conclusions about why some development projects were late or had quality problems:

- Engineers said the materials procurement system was wrong, and that their computer showed materials in the inventory that were not actually there. They didn't trust the ordering system, so they sometimes ordered things they didn't really need yet, "just to be sure they're available when we need them." This led to excess inventory that slowed the process of getting equipment.

- The inventory manager said, "Engineers keep telling us their numbers in inventory don't match ours, but that's because they are looking at the items marked for future jobs as if the material was already gone. It's not gone—it's just reserved for an upcoming job. They need to learn how to use the system and stop ordering things they don't plan to use."

- Installers said the engineer's maps were out of date, so they used their own maps to do work on job sites. They also said sometimes they didn't even take the engineers' maps out to the site with them because "they've got bad information on them that just messes us up." Resolving conflicting map information was one cause of delays.

- The computer operations team said, "Those three late jobs? We never saw the work requests for those projects until after the work was already done. Somebody in either engineering or installation forgot to make up the work orders when the job was authorized, or maybe the person did it and just forgot to hit 'send' when he or she was done. Those jobs were late because they didn't let everybody know as soon as the job dates were finalized. The prep crews could have been out there setting up the transformers so the installers could have come in on time."

Their detective work had given Alex and Tony more than just clues about job delays. They discovered an ongoing argument between engineers and inventory managers, heard an old and popular story about the outdated maps, and learned about the previously unknown role of the computer operations team in getting work order information to the right people at the right time.

Ultimately, the reason for job delays was that the engineers did not all put the work orders into the database the same way. That problem was easy to fix. The computer operations supervisor wrote up a five-step procedure, gave a copy to each engineer, and posted other copies on the walls in both engineering and installation areas. They held a meeting to demonstrate the proper way to enter a work order, emphasizing the importance of filling out all the fields and entering

it into the system as soon as the job was authorized.

These Understanding Conversations had solved
the problem, and there would not be any more
late jobs unless there were exceptional circumstances like weather or emergencies.

The bonus was that Alex and Tony also found
other things they could improve. They asked the
inventory manager to give the engineers a tutorial
on what each inventory computer screen was used
for and which ones they should use in planning
their jobs. They also contacted the city's mapping
technology manager and asked for help in getting
their maps up to date throughout the electricity
department.

The process of getting so many people involved in solving the mystery of the late jobs had
a high payoff. Everyone had a comment, many
people had complaints, and some people had good
ideas for how to solve the problem. Darryl discovered hidden connections between groups that were
the keys to improving communication. People in
the department said later that they enjoyed the
quest, and were glad to get to the bottom of
something instead of just blaming the people at
the other end of the building. The biggest reward
was that everyone knew their team had played a
part.

"Getting us involved in the process of figuring
this out was great, " one employee said. "We all

learned something about the way we need to work together. I used to think I understood my job, but now that I see how my work relates to everybody else, I understand it better than I did before."

The Limits of Understanding

The Alchemy of Shoulds, Coulds, and Complaints

Three forms of communication—shoulds, coulds, and complaints—lack a critical ingredient that prevents them from being useful. They do not include a commitment to get things right, but instead focus on what is wrong or whose fault it is. None of these three forms of communication can be treated as a harmless request for understanding. They are special communications that require special treatment.

- A complaint is a grievance that expresses pain, displeasure, and annoyance, and finds fault with people or situations, but it lacks an intention or commitment to do something about it.

- A "should" implies an obligation, as in, "You should get to work on time" or "I should get a good performance evaluation." Shoulds, and their first cousin, "oughts, " have a moral tone that appeals to what is right, proper, or appropriate. It is a passive complaint—the person speaking is not obligating himself to take action to make things right.

- A "could" is also used to suggest a possible course of action, as in, "I could get a higher commission if I focused on larger companies, " or "The stock could rise after the merger is complete." Coulds have no moral undertone, but they are uncommitted expressions of speculation or wishful thinking.

No initiative is launched by saying, "Americans should send a man to the moon." Someone in a position to make good on the commitment had to state that commitment, as Kennedy did when he said, "I believe we should commit ourselves to this goal, " and he asked others to add their commitment as well. The addition of commitment makes all the difference. Similarly, nothing gets started by saying, "We could open new bank branches across the state." When someone says, "We are going to open five new branches this year, and I am forming a team to determine the best timing for each location, " that person has created an initiative.

Complaints, shoulds, and coulds tend to arise in Understanding Conversations, and they can be useful forms of conversation only when they are treated, or reframed, as a possibility or an idea for making improvements. During an Understanding Conversation, you can accept complaints, shoulds, and coulds by reframing them. Recast them as potential contributions to the discussion, or as starting points for a solution to the problem they have identified.

Cathy, the Auto Town CEO, received a comment on one of the communication cards that said, "I want management to know that there is a pay discrepancy in our office. The administrative staff earns less than the repair schedulers, and ours is the only location where that is true."

"I didn't know what to do with this communication, " Cathy said, "partly because it was so off the topic of the purpose for the meeting, but mostly because I knew it was not true. All the locations have the same pay scales, and this was either a troublemaker or someone who didn't know the facts."

"When we went to the meeting, "she told us,"I told everyone that if they had any concerns about pay scales and discrepancies, they should communicate that with our HR office. Then the HR manager spoke for a few minutes in every Q&A meeting, adding an outline of a plan for a 'pay scale committee'with representatives from all eight locations. The committee would review the pay scales and make recommendations to the management team.

"The HR manager closed that part of his presentation by saying, 'Anyone who would like to get this committee going should contact me. Here is my phone number and email address, and I look forward to hearing from you.' He never heard from anyone, and a month later he sent out a memo to everyone in the company. The memo said: 'The pay scale committee idea has been cancelled due to lack of interest. If anyone has a concern about pay discrepancies, please let me know, and I will handle it.'"

The best solution for a complaint is to have people spell out the details needed for resolution. Put it back in their laps by asking them to take action or talk to someone who can do something about it.

- Ask the complainer to create an initiative: *What,*exactly, do we need to do or produce? *When*do we want that to happen? *Why*will it matter? These questions can turn a complaint into an initiative.

- Then ask the complainer: *Who*will do the work? *Where*will the resources come from? *How*will the work get done?

Of course, some complainers may be unwilling to commit themselves to answering those questions, but the process makes the point. Complaints, vague accusations, and hypothetical ideals are not a contribution to Understanding Conversations. Left untreated, they can sabotage progress and good will. If you are unable to have people add commitment to their shoulds, coulds, and complaints, then you must refer them to someone who can, and close the books on that conversation.

"I Don't Understand"—Possibility or Pretense?

Understanding does not mean every question gets answered or every individual is fully satisfied with all aspects of the situation or the plan. When, after a robust Understanding Conversation, some people still say, "I don't understand, " what are they really saying? There are three possibilities to consider.

After a discussion, some people may genuinely have some specific questions they want answered. If the answers are not available, or if the questions are inappropriate for the occasion, you can promise to follow up later. Then, in the followup, either provide the information or defuse the inappropriate question. When there are no answers for some questions, the best options are either to say so, and let people know when the information will be available, or invite them to contribute their suggestions.

Some people may not have specific questions, but are simply troubled by a vague discomfort regarding the unknowns that have now appeared in their futures. In many cases, the only reassurance is to let them know that Understanding Conversations will continue even after the project is underway, and provide some form of Q&A format for them to pose their questions and resolve their concerns as things progress. Monthly meetings, suggestion boxes, or order-in lunches can be the occasions to update Understanding Conversations as work progresses toward the goal.

Finally, some people say, "I do not understand" as a ploy to slow down or derail a proposed course of action. They may understand perfectly well the proposal's implications for their job and choose to avoid new responsibilities or communications. They may be afraid that they will not perform as expected in a new situation, be embarrassed, or miss out on a promotion. In some cases, people's desire to impede the progress of an initiative is a simple matter of trying to maintain existing relationships among coworkers.

Pretending not to understand can slow things down for everyone. To avoid getting into the quicksand of explanation, keep your attention on letting other people participate, supporting the *Who-Where-How* elements of the Understanding Conversation, and calling for everyone to take responsibility for finding solutions. When all else fails, set a time limit to the conversation and promise to return to the subject later when you have more ideas and solutions.

Understanding Does Not Mean Acceptance

Lucy, one of Jeffrey's MBA students, was upset about the grade she received on an exam question. After class, she asked, "Would you please reread this question? I think you may not have completely understood my answer."

"Ok, " he replied, and reread the exam question and Lucy's answer. On finishing, he said, "I don't see anything different from when I first read it. I don't see any reason to change your grade."

With this Lucy was even more agitated, asking, "Please read it one more time. I am sure the answer is appropriate, and I want you to understand it."

Reluctantly, Jeffrey reread the answer, then said, "Lucy, I have read your answer twice and told you my understanding of what you said. You say you want me to understand your answer, and I believe I do, but you don't think so. How would you know if I did understand?"

Lucy replied, "I think if you understood my answer, you would agree with it, and then you would change my grade."

"Well I do understand your answer. But I do not accept your answer. It is not an appropriate response to the question, and I am not changing the grade."

Understanding does not mean agreement, appreciation, or acceptance. Do not look for people to be happy and excited as proof of their understanding. In fact, when they understand the new idea, and consider their role in making it a reality, some people may choose not to participate and decide to go elsewhere. Instead, look for a willingness to engage in the conversation, and a willingness to help find answers to the questions that arise.

Kate and Mitch learned something about this when they finished their meeting about the HR-ITS schedule and performance measures. Kate was very pleased that so many people had contributed ideas about how to make the measures more meaningful. She felt they had made real progress toward agreeing on how to calculate useful results every month. Noticing the increasing level of enthusiasm as the meeting progressed, she confidently asked the group, "How many of you are satisfied with the idea of using these measures?"

"I expected almost every hand to go up, " she said later. "But only three people raised their hands. I had to ask them why there weren't more hands up, since they seemed so engaged in the conversation."

Finally, one person spoke up and said, "These measures will work well, but none of us wants to be accountable for reaching the goals you will set."

Kate told us, "I never once mentioned goals, but that is what they were thinking about. Their enthusiasm was only about being able to be part of setting the measures, but they were still uneasy about actually using them."

The only way some people become fully comfortable with new initiatives is by getting into action. The Understanding Conversation can bring them into the plan, but it won't necessarily make them happy. As people start testing and practicing their new roles, and realize they can continue to ask questions and contribute their ideas, some, if not most of the uneasiness will dissolve.

Understanding Does Not Cause Action

One of the biggest mistakes we make is to assume that when people understand something, they will take the appropriate actions. In fact, even perfect understanding does not cause, or necessarily encourage, action. One example to make this clear is our physical fitness. We all understand what to do to maintain a healthy weight and fitness level. Eat lightly, work out heartily three times a week, and see your doctor for regular checkups. We also know that for many people, a thorough understanding of these "rules" does not propel them into a regimen of fitness-producing actions. Understanding is

For this reason, Understanding Conversations can be potential black holes of communication where we linger too long, expecting action to arise spontaneously. Believing that understanding will precipitate action, we work harder to make people understand. We explain. We send them to trainings. We explain some more. This is like talking louder to a person who speaks another language. We need to recognize when it is time to move people into action-producing conversations (see Chapter 4). Understanding Conversations produce understanding, not action.

In their article

They go on to say, "But all that talking was just hot air. In 1989, a Harvard Business School case study on the project revealed that few concrete decisions had been made to change the quality of the company's products. There had been very little change in the attitudes of Xerox's managers toward quality. Nor had beliefs and behaviors been altered—for instance, only 15% of Xerox employees said they believed that recognition and rewards were based on improvements in quality, and only 13% reported using cost of quality analyses in their decision making."

Many leaders who want to implement new ideas assume the place to begin is by changing the knowledge and attitudes of individuals. Changes in attitudes, the theory goes, will lead to changes in behavior, and behavioral changes repeated by many people will result in organizational change.[5] This theory may account, at least in part, for the large number of organization change failures. The temptation to keep working on trying to have people *understand* can delay or prevent us from moving into Performance Conversations.

If You Are Missing Understanding Conversations

Understanding Conversations can be difficult to facilitate and navigate, especially because they require the input of people who may be upset, threatened by, or opposed to a proposed initiative. As a result, these

108

conversations are an opportunity to learn whether your listening skills need to be developed, or if you should bring in facilitators to support you in the discussions.

Gaining people's commitment to participate in developing and implementing a plan is the one element that will be most important for success, so it is helpful to practice several different ways to have and support Understanding Conversations.

If You Don't Use Understanding Conversations

Resistance to implementing a new idea usually surprises the people who draft strategic plans and change initiatives. Just as Kate and Mitch did not expect to encounter arguments about their well-designed metrics, managers may be caught off guard by discovering that most people do not like being told what to do. Instead, people want to be part of the "in crowd" that helps to design a change and have the chance to get their opinions in at the planning phase. Understanding Conversations are the way to give people that opportunity, before every decision has been made and carved in stone.

Without Understanding Conversations, leaders can face a quiet revolution that will bog them down in attempts to motivate, educate, and otherwise enlighten people who are simply not interested in listening. The resources expended on getting people engaged in a new project can include everything from expensive off-site retreats and entertainments to new technologies and training programs, redesigned compensation systems, or new employee facilities and services. Instead, a well-designed Understanding Conversation can work to engage people in adding substantive improvements into a proposed initiative, and perhaps avoid some costly mistakes.

If You Use Them Improperly

Using all six elements will ensure that you drive up all the questions and all the possible contributions people have for improving the proposed initiative. Start with the

You can expect people will begin asking you questions about each of those elements (Why do you want that? Can it be done by that time? Why do you really want it?), but they will soon start working with you to address some version of the other three questions:

A big problem with any Understanding Conversation is the trap of dealing with disagreement and resistance. People who have complaints, or who persistently point out the reasons an initiative will fail, can make a tempting target to many leaders. The temptation is to set these people straight, explain why they misunderstand, and give them facts and optimistic projections. If that tactic is pursued too long, the topic of discussion will no longer be about the initiative, but about whether certain people approve of the idea or are willing to engage in a productive conversation.

These discussions can go wrong in many ways, as when they are dominated by people who want attention focused on their own agenda (e.g., for improving their position or enhancing their reputation). Discussions can also be weighed down by a single argument that goes on too long, or by persistent questions on matters that cannot be addressed now. The cost of these problems is usually only that they slow down the process, but losing the valuable time of so many people in a major initiative can be expensive.

Finally, leaders who expect one or two unstructured Q&A sessions to propel people into action will also be disappointed. As the examples of the Auto Town CEO and the electricity managers demonstrate, there are different ways to conduct Understanding Conversations. They all, however, require at least some preparation time and attention to decisions such as who can be involved, what questions will be highlighted, and what answers are most accurate, informative, and engaging.

Your ability to keep the goal in mind is an important factor in the success of Q&A or other types of Understanding Conversation meetings. Your goal is to give and gain information, and to engage people in contributing ideas that are likely to support the eventual implementation of the initiative. Remembering this goal and being a good listener will help steer you through an effective Understanding Conversation.

If You Use Too Many Understanding Conversations

Staying too long in Understanding Conversations is a common mistake, as most people believe sufficient understanding will trigger effective action. This error can cost momentum and people, because those who "buy in" early become impatient as they wait for the reluctant few to get on board. Explanations become boring for the go-getters, and they may move on to other activities.

It is more effective to have a few Q&A sessions and move into Performance Conversations (see Chapter 4) than to risk stagnation in the understanding phase. Understanding Conversations can be built into an ongoing communication structure, with weekly, monthly, or quarterly status meetings or "town hall" Q&A sessions. Leaders who have an "open door policy" are another example of providing an opportunity for ongoing Understanding Conversations, as are well-monitored suggestion boxes or intranet discussion groups.

Putting It into Practice

Start by reminding people of the initiative. You can use the statement developed in the Initiative Conversation, but remember that one outcome of Understanding Conversations is that you might change the way you say what you want. Adding the language and ideas of the various participants in Understanding Conversations is a beneficial improvement for a proposed initiative, and increases its chances of success. Understanding Conversations are the opportunity to update the table you drafted during your Initiative Conversations to develop a more comprehensive and complete plan for accomplishing your initiative:

List of Initiatives

What Is the Result or Outcome We Want?	When Do We Want It? (Be as specific as you can)	Why Do We Want It? (State the difference that it will make)
1		
2		
3		

Table 4

Invite people to talk, and ask them to help you translate unproductive comments into productive ones. In addition to upgrading your initiative statement, you also want to capture information to create a new version of *Who-Where-How,* shown in the table below. When you engage people in a conversation of the specific ways to fulfill an initiative, you are asking about *Who* will do the work, *Where* the resources are, and *How* the work will be done. These are all subjects people will have ideas and opinions about, and they will want their ideas to be heard. And you want to hear those ideas to gain strength and accuracy for a more complete plan. You can capture a list of their recommendations using a whiteboard or easel tablet, which will let them see that their ideas are being recorded, reinforcing that you are listening.

For Each Initiative

Who Will Do the Work?	Where Will Resources Come From?	How Will the Work Get Done?
1		
2		
3		

Table 5

Practicing Understanding Conversations is a process of having appointments and meetings to present the

Chapter Four

Performance Conversations: Ask and Promise

Brian learned the power of specific requests when he asked Sam, a new consultant who had been with Sys-Tek Consulting less than nine months, to turn over the management of a new account he had spent months cultivating. Even though it was a large and complex account that went beyond his experience, Sam had been reluctant to turn over the account to anyone else. Then Brian took a performance approach in his conversation with Sam:

"Sam, you and I have had numerous discussions about the new account, and as you may recall, I originally wanted you to turn over its management to one of the senior consultants because I thought it was more than you could handle."

"Yes, I recall your initial concern. But, at the time, the client's relationship was with me, he trusted me, and he wanted me in charge."

Brian said, "That's right, and for that reason I have left you in charge. But since then, it has come to my attention that you are falling behind on some key deliverables. This risks our client's satisfaction and could impact Sys-Tek's reputation."

"It's true. I am behind, but I will get caught up this week."

"Sam, during the past several weeks I have tried to get you to understand that it is time that you turn over the account. I have talked to you about the importance of teamwork and working with other consultants, and the need to bring in other Sys-Tek experts when dealing with a complex contract like this one. I even kidded you about being 'someone who likes scaling cliffs barehanded' at one of our staff meetings, thinking a little embarrassment might prompt you to make the transfer."

Sam was surprised, saying, "Wow, I had no idea all that was about you wanting me to turn the account over. I thought your comment about teamwork was a reminder to get others involved, so I did that. And I thought your comment about 'scaling cliffs' was a compliment on my willingness to face big challenges. I had no idea you were still concerned about my ability to handle this client."

"Well, I'm no longer going to be indirect. I am asking you to turn over the account to Jules by the close of business today. I told him I would be asking you to do this and asked that he make himself available to you. He agreed, and you can find him in his office until 6:00 tonight."

Brian continued, "I know that what I'm asking you to do is difficult, but if you accept my request, I promise you will remain the client's primary contact person, and the client will not notice any real difference in the project communications. You will also get 50% management credit for this contract and full commission credit for any additional follow-up work. This is more than any other consultant would get, but you have done a reasonably good job with a complex project, and I want that acknowledged. Still, it is time to make the change. Do you accept my request?"

Sam accepted, saying, "Of course I'll turn the account over to Jules. I will meet with him this afternoon and bring him up to date. And I appreciate and accept your promise for credits. It is very generous."

Brian was relieved. "Good. I will follow up with Jules and start the necessary paperwork for changing management credits this afternoon. Let's meet next Tuesday to see what issues remain and how best to move you into other projects."

Performance Conversations are made of requests and promises, and they result in agreements to take action and/or produce results. Brian went through several weeks of indirect and frustrating conversations that did not get him the result he wanted. When he finally made a specific request, he removed all ambiguity, and Sam was able to respond with a promise for action.

Performance Conversations are not the same thing as those once-or-twice-a-year "performance evaluations" that managers and supervisors give to their subordinates to let them know how they are doing. A performance evaluation is an assessment of how well an individual has performed over a past period of time. A Performance Conversation is not an assessment of the past; it is an agreement for the future.

Performance Conversations are specific agreements for *What* will be done, *When* it will be done, *Why* it matters, *Who* agrees to do it, *Where* the result will be delivered, and *How* things will be done. All six of the traditional journalist's questions come into play to create a "performance agreement" for taking action and producing results.

Commit to Performance: What-When-Why

Performance Conversations are designed to have people commit to performance (i.e., to take actions and produce results). For people who want to get things done through the actions of others, knowing how to get people moving is worth its weight in gold. How do we have people be responsible for their work? What has people do their jobs? The answer is: make good requests and get good promises.

The American Society of Training and Development (ASTD) conducted a study to determine under what conditions people are most likely to complete a task. Their results, summarized in the table below, indicate that people are most likely to complete tasks when they make a commitment to another person to do it. In fact, people are six times more likely to do something when they promise actions, results, or outcomes to someone else (65%) than when they just hear a good idea (10%).[1]

Table 6

Condition	Likelihood of Doing Task
If you hear an idea	10%
If you consciously decide to adopt it	25%
If you decide when you will do it	40%
If you plan how you will do it	50%
If you commit to someone else you will do it	65%
You have a specific accountability appointment with the person you have committed to	95%

These findings tell us that when we want people to take action and produce results, we have to ask them to do it, get their promise to do it, and follow up with them after they do it—or after they do not. Asking, promising, and following up are all parts of a Performance Conversation.

To support a commitment to action—your own and others'—you must specify

What-When-Why. What, exactly, do you want? *When* do you want it? *Why* does it matter? Performance Conversations get people into action.

This may sound like the recipe for an Initiative Conversation, but it is not. Initiative Conversations propose futures that have yet to be fully developed. They provide a general direction in which to move, a direction that must be "filled in" through Understanding Conversations. Performance Conversations are about specific actions and results to be produced by specific people with a specific time limit. There is nothing general about a Performance Conversation: the result is an individual who agrees to complete a specific subproject or task to support the success of a larger goal. Initiative Conversations are idea-generators; Performance Conversations are action-generators.

Commit Yourself First

When we think about the things we might do, could do, or would like to do, we are only having thoughts and are under no obligation to take action on any of them. Even if we invest time researching our options and drafting an action plan, though that might increase the likelihood of action, we still have no obligation to perform.

As soon as we tell someone, "I will do it, " however, we have made a promise. Someone else is counting on us, expecting something from us, and will be disappointed or in a difficult position if we do not take action. Our promise creates an obligation to take action and do what we said we would do. If we schedule an appointment for a date, time, and place to report on our actions and results, we create the opportunity to "account for" the promise. As shown in the ASTD study, when we must face the person to whom we have promised something, the likelihood we will keep our word is almost certain (95%).

If you want others to take action on your behalf, you will gain a strong foundation for making powerful requests by committing yourself first. Brian told us he used this tip to help himself to be direct with Sam. Before he confronted Sam, he met with one of Sys-Tek's principals and promised to transfer the new account to a more senior consultant.

> Brian said, "I had been frustrated ever since Sam landed that contract, afraid that he didn't have the experience to fulfill all our commitments to the client. But I didn't know how to get him to give it up until my boss told me he would honor any compensation plan I thought was fair. My boss directed me to get Sam off the lead position on the account, and I promised I would do it right away. At that point, I was on the hook to deliver the result."

Brian made a commitment to get the account transferred and then formulated his plan of action to accomplish it. His action plan was a list of requests and promises:

- A request to Jules that he take the role of project leader, and a promise from Jules that he would accept the request
- A request to Sam that he turn over the account, and a promise from Sam that he would do so
- A promise to Sam that he would be the client contact leader and would get half the management credit for the job
- A request to accounting that it change the allocation of management credits, and a promise from accounting that it would do so
- A request to his assistant that there be no change in the client contact records after Jules took over the account, and her promise to keep Sam on the record

Brian implemented his plan by having the Performance Conversations that would get everyone committed to taking new action. By telling Sam they would meet in a week to discuss any remaining issues, Brian also set up an appointment to follow through on the turnover. As part of completing this matter, Brian had a Closure Conversation (see Chapter 5) with Jules, accounting, and his assistant to be sure they had taken the actions they promised.

Saying Yes Is a Promise

A promise is a commitment by one person to another to do what they say they will do. You make a promise when you tell someone, "I will have the lawnmower sharpened by noon on Friday, " "I will call the vendor today and get them to commit to the delivery time, " or "I will sign the authorization this afternoon and priority mail it today, so you will have it tomorrow." You are now obligated to the other person to do what you promised, and, as ASTD's findings show, making this commitment has a substantial impact on your behavior.

FedEx once ran an advertisement showing a woman walking down a busy city street carrying a box. Prominently displayed on the box was the word FedEx. Under the woman's picture were the following words:

> Ours isn't the only name on the box. Amy's reputation is on the line. When her client asks if the contracts will arrive in the morning, Amy says "yes." Brave Amy, delving into the world of "yes." "Yes" raises the stakes. "Yes" comes with responsibility. There are no loopholes in "yes." Is Amy worried? No. Relax, it's FedEx.

Most delivery services, and many other businesses and agencies as well, make similar promises to do what they say they will do. Their obligation to keep their promise and deliver is heightened because their promises are very public. When a company fails to keep its promise, customers lose confidence in it, stop using its services, and perhaps complain about it to friends and colleagues.

The failure to keep promises can damage corporate reputations, but individual promises are equally visible, although to a smaller circle of friends and associates.

Each of us has a personal reputation with respect to our promise-keeping ability. You know people who are often late, or unprepared, or unreliable in the quality of their work—they have a reputation for that. They may not realize that saying yes is a promise, or that their word matters, but promises kept and promises broken are a vital indicator of the quality of relationships in every aspect of life.

Saying No Is Sometimes Necessary

Sometimes people say they will do something and then don't do it. We call this "saying yes, but doing no" because the promise was made, but the actions were not performed, and the results were not produced. In some cases, promises are broken for legitimate reasons, such as a computer system crash, planes delayed on snowy runways, or the illness of a coworker. In other cases, the reasons are less valid, such as when the failure is due to poor planning, incomplete communication, or a lack of intention. Whether the reasons are legitimate or not, there may be consequences for not keeping our word: we may impair other people's ability to deliver, cost extra time or money, or simply disappoint other people.

When confronted with a large or complicated request, it may be wise to say no until the resource issues, timetables, and communication requirements are spelled out and everyone involved fully understands what he or she is promising. Sometimes saying no is necessary because the resource availability is uncertain, or too many other outstanding commitments prevent rearrangement of schedules and communications. When people are depending on us to keep our word, it is better to admit immediately if we realize that we will be unable to finish the work as promised. As a rule, it is better to *say* no than to "say yes but do no."

Saying No Is Sometimes Necessary

A request is a mechanism for gaining a commitment from people to do or produce something. Whenever you assign a task to a team member, petition your boss for a plum project, or ask a colleague to meet you for lunch, you are using requests. There are many different types of requests:

- Invitations
- Instructions
- Requirements or specifications
- Orders or directives
- Commands or demands

These different ways of "asking" another person to do something for you will influence the relative strength or force of the request. Giving an order is more forceful than extending an invitation and, as a result, has a much different effect on the person receiving it. If you are speeding, and a police car pulls up behind you with lights flashing and siren wailing, technically speaking the officer is making a request that you pull over to the side of the road, but it is a forceful command, not an optional invitation.

A request is an invitation (or command) to take an action and includes a statement of

Mitch, the manager of the information technology systems (ITS) group, had been reluctant to ask his technicians to give up their homegrown system of scheduling and tracking ITS jobs. He anticipated resistance, believing they would be annoyed at having to take the time and trouble to learn the Work Order Scheduling system. Aside from not wanting to make the change, he feared they would think he had lost a battle with his peers over using the system. Mitch did not want the technicians to be angry, and he did not want them to think that he had failed them. But he had to make the switch to using the new system, so he had to break the news and get their buy-in.

"There is a new goal in this company, " he told them, "to have everyone in the organization using the Work Order Scheduling software to manage their own work. That includes us. Two other managers—and I won't say who they are—told me they did not think we could do this in our ITS department because we're too stubborn. I probably shouldn't have, but I told them not only could we do it, but also that we could do it in two weeks." He paused to hear the groans, and then went on. "So here's what I need from you. Tell me every reason you can think of why it can't be done."

They used the whiteboard and made the list of reasons, and, being technicians, promptly set about solving each item. The result was that they were using the new system within ten days. Mitch's request for action was framed as a *What-When-Why* communication: Start using the new work order system, do it within two weeks, and do it because other people said we can't. He challenged the technicians, and it worked.

What Do You Want?

Knowing what you want, and communicating it clearly, is the heart of a request. What you want is usually a job done: a result, outcome, or product. When you have a complex outcome or inexperienced people, you may need to break it down into manageable tasks, or even subtasks, that will "roll up" into the result you want. With experienced people, you may simply make the request for the result you want and let the people determine the specific ways to produce it.

Kirk, a new sales manager, made a request of his sales staff at their weekly meeting. He said, "We are starting a new campaign, and as part of its launch I want each of you to make at least 200 cold calls a week. That should generate a 10% increase in new leads."

After two weeks, Kirk saw no increase in new leads. Concerned, he dropped in on

Megan, one of the salespeople, and asked her if she was making the calls.

"Yes, I am, " she replied. "But I am not catching anyone in, so I am not actually talking to many people."

Kirk realized he had asked for the wrong result: he did not want his staff just making calls, he wanted them to talk to more prospects so they would generate more good leads. Seeing his mistake, Kirk changed his request at the next staff meeting.

"I see that asking you to make 200 cold calls each week had you focus on making calls instead of getting you to be more creative in finding new leads. After talking with Megan, I see what I really want is for you to have as many conversations as you need in order to produce a 10% increase in leads."

This new request prompted a brainstorming session about how to get new leads. Some of the ideas were to attend an upcoming business-networking seminar, put up a booth at a professional conference, and host a reception for local community leaders. Focusing on the desired result instead of restricting people to specific instructions encouraged new actions and outcomes.

When Do You Want It? Give and Get Deadlines.

A deadline is a powerful ingredient of a Performance Conversation. It creates immediacy, adds to the accountability for the promise, and increases certainty for everyone. If you don't know when you want the results, or if the timeline is not a critical part of your plan, then ask the person to whom you are making the request, "When can you have this done?" Asking the

Without a deadline or a "*When,*" people are left with a "whenever." That is when it will get done: "whenever" they get around to doing it, or "whenever" they have the time, or "whenever" you nag them enough. If you ever notice that you have to keep asking people for the results they promised, it is a reminder to add the *When*time element to your requests. If you have to nag and beg, your request has become a "whenever" on their list of things to do.

Some people believe deadlines are a source of stress, but uncertainty actually causes more stress than deadlines. Deadlines help people plan their work and manage their time and other resources. If people do not know when something is due, it also reduces the effectiveness of their communication with others. Look at your own "to do" list. How many items have a due date associated with them? And how many of those same items are a nagging source of concern?

To reduce uncertainty, use specific deadlines: January 19 is a specific example. Saying "mid-January, " "as soon as possible, " "when you get a chance, " or "next week" is not specific. A clear and unambiguous deadline adds certainty. For example, "The wireless program report is to be handed over to the vice president by 3:30 PM, January 19" is obvious and certain, and allows everyone to plan all the tasks required to make that final result a reality.

No fake deadlines. When you give and get deadlines, they need to be real ones. Giving false deadlines, where you set the due date earlier than you really need it, risks your credibility and reduces people's willingness to meet your deadlines in the future.

Martine, a research biologist, has had more than her share of deadlines set artificially early. She still remembers her former boss who set a Thursday afternoon "do-or-die" deadline for a research report. Martine met the deadline, and when she went to his office to drop off the report at 3:30 PM on Thursday, she discovered he had already left for the day, and he would be out of the office both Friday and the following Monday. "Nobody took his deadlines seriously after that, " she said. "He never apologized, but no matter what excuse he would have given, it wouldn't have been good enough. People don't like being fooled."

Why Does it Matter? People Need a Context

You have your reasons for making a particular request, but if you do not say what they are, the person you ask to do the work will hear only a task, not an opportunity. People do better work when they understand the importance of a request, or see that it relates to a particular initiative, goal, or objective. If we do not add any context, all we leave them with is "Do this and hurry up about it, " which is not a strong foundation for a performance agreement.

When you help people see that their work matters, and that what they are doing contributes to larger goals, they are more attentive to producing whatever you need to help reach your goals. Just as giving a deadline lets people know there is some urgency to your request, telling them why your request matters gives them a framework for understanding and adjusting priorities.

Yes, You Have To Ask

Do you really have to ask people to do things? Can't people see for themselves what needs to be done? Don't they understand what their jobs are?

Yes. No. No.

You really do have to say, "I request that you do X, by Y, for Z."

X = What action, result, or outcome you want, including all its specifications

Y = When the due date and time that you want it are

Z = Why it is important to you, the organization, or another higher goal or context

For example, Brian's request of Sam was "I request you turn over the account to Jules by the close of business today so he can get started." Other examples are, "I'm asking that you complete the audit and have it in the new format by noon tomorrow so we can use it as a handout in the afternoon meeting, " and "I propose we meet for lunch Tuesday at Applebee's at our usual time. Since we'll be finalizing my project requirements, lunch is my treat."

We cannot assume that people always know *What* we want, *When* we want it, and *Why* it matters, without making clear requests and promises. People can see actions or jobs that could—or should—be done, but do not necessarily jump to the conclusion that they are the ones who should be responsible for doing them. They may believe they need permission from someone else, or more guidance, or a different level of decision authority. Alternatively, they may just not want to take the actions, or do not want to be responsible for making the decision to act.

Furthermore, people are busy and may feel they are behind in their workload. Unless you make requests, and ask people to commit to doing a certain job with a specific timeline, they will make up their own decisions about what to work on and when. They will use their priority system instead of yours. As the ASTD study shows, people are more likely to do something when they have made a commitment to someone, and the best way to get a commitment from someone is to make a request for "

Promises Create Agreements: Who-Where-How

Virtually everything done in an organization is done because people make requests and honor their promises. But, as Brian discovered in his interactions with Sam, and as Kirk discovered with his staff, people don't always ask for what they want in a way that other people can do the task. If we do not make a good request, we will not receive a good promise, which means we have no agreement to get work done or results produced.

Responses to a Request and Pathways to a Promise

If you are a boss, people will tend to accept your requests because they think the potential consequences of saying no could affect their reputations and careers. If you are not a boss, you may believe you have to accept all requests that come your way, especially if they come from someone "higher up" than you are.

The strength of a request is influenced by who makes it, the potential consequences of accepting or declining, and the willingness of the listener to accept those consequences. For many of us, requests from a boss are stronger than requests from coworkers, customers, and vendors. No matter what your position, it is good to remember there are three options when it comes to a request: you can accept, decline, or counteroffer.

Accept. To accept a request is to say yes, which is making a promise to do what is asked. When people take a moment to hear, consider, and accept a request, there is a much greater likelihood that they will keep their promise than if we just toss the request on their desk and expect them to do it. In the interest of high-quality work and time-sensitive results, not to mention satisfied coworkers, after someone gives you a yes, it is wise to confirm that he or she recognizes he or she has just made a promise, and confirm that the person intends to invest the time and resources to keep his or her word. Saying yes is promising the actions, results, and timelines, which means you have an agreement for performance, and you know exactly when to follow up.

Decline. To decline a request is to say, "No, I am not going to do that for you." For most of us, declining a request, especially face-to-face, is uncomfortable, even when we are not worried about negative consequences. As a result, we rarely hear people say no to a request. We are more likely to hear some kind of hedging such as, "Let me think about it, " "OK, but I can't get to it right away, " or "Can you get back to me on that?"

When people feel they cannot say no to a request, they may accept the request and then not do the task. This is the "say yes but do no" situation. A good way to avoid that is to let people know you prefer them to decline your requests if they cannot arrange their time and resources to give you a good promise.

People may be able to decline an invitation, but orders and commands have far greater consequences. Failing to pull over for the police can eventually get you arrested. Failing to accept an invitation to have a piece of dark chocolate that is 84% cocoa will not get you arrested. Make sure you clarify whether your request is an invitation or a demand.

If someone declines your request, he or she has refused to make a promise. This may be an opportunity to try to remove the obstacles to the person's promises. You can do this by clarifying the specifics of *Who* else would be available to provide support, *Where* the resources are, or *How* the work might get done. Sometimes when people decline a request, they are willing to reconsider when they know more about it. People are reluctant to promise for a variety of reasons, but the primary two include:

a) They do not believe that the necessary resources will be available in a timeline that ensures they will be able to keep their promise. If you want them to promise, you'll have to work with them on the resource issues.

b) They are not confident that they can produce *What* is wanted *When* you want it, either due to a concern about their own capacities, or about external factors they believe will impair their performance. We know one manager who refused to give a presentation to his company's purchasing staff because he was required to include information about how the accounting system handled taxation of uniforms for the company's truck drivers. He didn't want to offend the union members, who disagreed with the corporate taxation policy, and he declined the request to give the presentation.

In both cases, the person making the request has two options. One is to accept that the other person has declined the request and will not perform the tasks or produce the results, in which case there is no promise. The second is to have a discussion to review and possibly revise the specifics of the job, timeline, and purpose

Counteroffer. A counteroffer is a proposal to modify the request. "I can't have it by Monday, but I could have it by Wednesday. Will that still work for you?" The counteroffer opens a negotiation to change the deadline, adjust the resources, or alter something about the action or outcome requested. Counteroffers have the value of encouraging everyone in the conversation to take a closer look at the details of the request and the costs of its fulfillment. If the request can be revised to everyone's satisfaction, you have a promise.

Who Can Promise? Ask the Right People

Requests can only be fulfilled by people who are in a position to fulfill them. Seems obvious, right?

Paul needed a financial report for last quarter's sales results, and he wanted it broken out by individual sales representatives. He went to the manager of the accounting department and described the report at length, detailing all the specific attributes he wanted itemized. Then he explained his reasons for needing the report, and emphasized that he would keep the information confidential. He talked for several minutes, and finally made the request. "Would you print me a copy of that?"

The manager said, "I would be happy to, but I am not the one who handles those things. The reports are produced in the finance office, so you'll have to talk with Marie."

Not everyone is in a position to make a promise for every action or outcome. In many cases, we know the right person to ask to get what we want. But in those cases where we don't, or where we are uncertain, it saves time to ask, "I am interested in X. Are you the one I should talk to?" People who can make promises are people who are willing to commit to producing a result.

You can accept someone's promise as his or her commitment to perform only if you remind the person that you expect him or her to keep his or her word, and that you will follow up with the person to see that he or she did. Telling your golfing buddy, "I am going to increase my sales next month" may be of interest to your buddy, but it is not a promise. He is not likely to follow up on whether you kept your word. Telling your boss you are going to increase your sales, however, is different because he or she has a keen interest in your performance in that area.

People are more likely to act if they make the promise to someone who genuinely cares about whether they perform. The *Who* of making a promise, in order to establish an agreement, has two sides: *Who* is promising, and *Who* is accepting the promise. When both parties have a clear statement of *What* is expected, *When* it is due, and *Why* it is important, there are promises on both sides: one to deliver, and one to follow up and provide support. We will have more to say about follow-up in Closure Conversations (Chapter 5).

Where Will the Resources and Deliverables Be?

Clarifying the
There are many *Wheres*associated with your requests and promises, and some of them will matter more than others. Sometimes even simple things need to be stated. Where is the meeting? Where do people want to be called—in their offices or on their mobile phones? Where will the final product be delivered?

What does it cost when good results are delivered to the wrong person at the wrong place? We know of one instance where hundreds of training manuals (costing thousands of dollars) met all the requirements of the request except that they were delivered to the wrong city. We also recall the time someone took a plane to Columbus, Ohio, instead of Columbus, Georgia, which turned out to be an expensive mistake.

How Will the Job Get Done?

A cliché says, "If you want something done, give it to a busy person." This suggests that busy people are somehow magically able to accept requests and make promises, and will be able to deliver as needed.

When it comes to Performance Conversations, a more appropriate saying might be, "If you want something done, give it to someone who will complete it." This means giving it to someone who meets three criteria. First, the person is able and knowledgeable enough to sketch out a checklist or work plan for how he or she will fulfill the request. Second, the person is, or will be, available to do what you ask. Finally, the person is willing to make the promise to satisfy the request.

Many people don't like making work plans, even simple lists of things to do. We have heard more than one person say, "In the time it takes to create a plan, I could have the job done." Nobody needs to use project management software for a single task or a small job that can be defined on a medium-size sticky note. But with some assignments, there are questions that need to be answered about the job to give people who are making a promise the confidence that they will, in fact, be able to get it done to meet the time and content specifications.

After-the-fact excuses such as "I didn't have the staff I needed for the job, " "We had to go with the lowest bidder, and he didn't have the top-notch skill set we needed, " or "Our financial office was preoccupied with payroll when we needed it to do record searches" are symptoms of an incomplete Performance Conversation. Take the time to determine what resources are required to fulfill your request and whether they are available on the timeline you need in order to get a good promise.

Scheduled availability. Being available means the person making the promise can schedule the time he or she will need to do the work outlined in the checklist or plan. If there is no checklist or work plan, the promise may be hollow: someone is saying yes to an unspecified set of actions. It is not safe to assume people can (or should) find the time, or that people are excellent managers of their schedules. Your job is to gain confidence that you are getting a good promise. With a plan and a schedule, you can prevent upsets and emergencies later.

The point of referring to a work plan and a schedule is not to micromanage the person making the promise, but to create confidence about the promise. Most of us have a tendency to overestimate what we can do, and we underestimate the problems we are likely to encounter. By talking though the plans for doing a job, handling resources, and balancing the schedule, we reduce the impact of those tendencies and increase the likelihood of success.

A good promise. When someone creates or accepts a plan of action, including resource management, and has scheduled the time to do the work, the person can make a good promise. This establishes an agreement—you know who will do the job and when to follow up to keep things on course toward a successful conclusion. All of the elements of Performance Conversations are at work, and you have an agreement to make something happen.

Confirm the Agreement—Your Expectations Are Not Their Promises

Some people make promises, even when they lack confidence or are aware of potential obstacles. Some make a promise even when they have doubts about it, either out of fear or overconfidence. Many people are reluctant to counteroffer, because they are unwilling to ask for a change in the timeline, requirements, or resources.

Worse, however, is that some people accept promises from those people, knowing they have not confirmed all the elements of a Performance Conversation. Why? Because conducting Performance Conversations properly takes more time and attention than they want to give.

The time it takes to plan and conduct an effective Performance Conversation is a good investment in productivity and satisfaction for your workplace. When we leave a Performance Conversation with some things that we "hoping" will be fulfilled, but have not made them explicit, we are undermining our own success. Hidden expectations undermine a good agreement between the requester and the promiser.

It saves time in the end to have a conversation in which you debrief people to confirm that you have an agreement. The debrief conversation is a simple review of the *What-When-Why* of the request and the *Who-Where-How* of the promise. You want a good promise that works for everyone and an agreement you can trust.

Manage the Agreement

Performance Conversations can be a lever for accomplishment and a foundation for accountability. This is true only when the person who makes the request, gathers the promises, and confirms the agreements, is also willing to be the manager of the agreements. Performance agreements put everyone involved on the hook for accomplishing something. The person who manages the agreement is the one who will keep the agreement in existence until it is either fulfilled or terminated, and who will make it easy for others to remember their part of the bargain.

Help People Remember

People forget things, including their agreements with other people. Forgetting is expensive: it costs delays, missed opportunities, and unfulfilled promises, so it is good to find ways to help people remember.

Chandra, a public relations coordinator for a large community organization, tells us, "I have a lot of community contacts to manage, but my biggest challenge is that they all want our department managers and technical specialists to come and speak to their civic group or their charity or church. So I am always going back to our people and asking them to give a talk or make an appearance at outside events. I have learned that I need to help them remember they have agreed to do this."

"Sometimes I watch someone put the date in his calendar. Then I ask him, "How much time do you need to prepare your presentation?"He always looks at me like I'm a genius for remembering that he will have to do that, but then I stay in his office until I see that he has blocked out the necessary time in his office calendar to develop his presentation. Then I send him an email three weeks before the event, then two weeks before, then one week before. From then on, I am in touch with him at least two more times before the event."

"I want people to be successful, and if they are not ready, they will not be so willing to do it again in the future. It was hard to realize I needed to do all that, but now I have a system and it is almost transparent for me. If I want other people to do things, I need to be responsible for providing the support structure so we all win."

The most common reason people forget to work on a promise is that they did not put the timeline in their calendars or schedule the time to do the work to meet the due dates. The second most common reason people forget is that they encounter an obstacle requiring unexpected time to resolve and then set the work aside. They promise themselves to get back to it later, but every time they think about returning to the task, the obstacle comes to mind, and they postpone the action again.

This kind of distraction and delay can be resolved by helping people remember. Remind them to put things in their calendars. Remind them to schedule the work. Tell them to contact you when they run into obstacles. As the manager of the agreement, you are responsible to see that all elements of the Performance Conversation are present for all other parties to the agreement.

Make Promises Public

People are more likely to do what they say when there are plenty of witnesses. Most of us want to be respected, well thought of, and seen as credible, so when our promises are made public we have a lot at stake in keeping our word. Making our promises public increases ownership as well as opportunities for support.

One way to make a promise public is by using a display such as the United Way thermometer. Or you can announce the promises, commitments, or agreements at a meeting or post a display on a bulletin board. When the display is maintained to stay current and accurate, everyone can tell at a glance how things are going. A public announcement or display encourages people to talk about, and act in, support of the goal.

Not every promise is appropriate for public display. Some promises, such as those involving financial or personnel decisions, may be sensitive or must be kept confidential. But in most workplace meetings it is appropriate to make a record of every time someone agrees to do something, and note what the person will do and when he or she will do it. Going a step farther to post certain promises for team outcomes also helps focus attention on the desired results.

It can take courage to go public with promises, because it makes both success and failure visible. In part, that is the reason to do it. Public displays bring successes and failures into the view of people who are interested in improving the group's performance. It also sets people up to have more effective Closure Conversations (Chapter 5).

If You Are Missing Performance Conversations

We can see why Performance Conversations are the least developed of all four types of conversation. Accountability has two sides: we cannot hold someone accountable for a result unless we ourselves are accountable for setting up the promise and supporting the agreement. Until we gain experience in doing this, it can seem like a lot of work. Eventually, it becomes a work habit that is easy to use.

Chandra told us, "The first time a department manager failed to show up at an event I had organized, I realized I would have to manage people in keeping their agreements with me. These were people who did not report to me, and in most cases were much higher up in the organization than I am. How could I 'manage' them?"

I had to learn how to make agreements that I knew they would keep. These are busy people who are already doing a lot of things, so if I want them to do something for me, I have to find a way to make that easy for them to remember and a positive experience to perform. I'm a master at making agreements now, but I made a lot of mistakes before I got it right."

Performance Conversations are the lever for causing action. They create agreements for actions and results, and they make unspoken or vague commitments visible and actionable. Every project, program, and implementation requires a combination of requests and promises over time in order to move people out of simply thinking about what to do and into taking committed action. The person who masters Performance Conversations has acquired a very powerful skill for getting people to move into action and producing results.

If You Don't Use Performance Conversations

The biggest mistake we make with Performance Conversations is not recognizing that we need them. We think we should not have to ask, or we believe that people already know what to do. Those are not good assumptions. As our friend TJ says, "People think work gets done 'automagically, ' as if you just have to think something and it will be done. Not true. It takes a lot to produce results." We like the word "automagically"—it summarizes the vague wishes we have when we don't use Performance Conversations.

Most people appear to be busy, but that does not mean they are productive. Without the rigor of specific requests and promises, people will go through the motions, doing what they habitually do, what they think they should do, or nothing at all. Well-designed Performance Conversations can clarify people's assignments so that they are not confused about priorities ("What should I be working on now?"), uncertain about when things are due ("When do they want this?"), or resentful ("How do they expect me to do all of this?").

We need Performance Conversations to clarify responsibilities and give people the opportunity to contribute to a goal. This means we must invest the time and attention to frame our expectations as requests that others can fulfill. We also need to support people in making promises that will help them to be productive and make good use of their time. People who are working to meet expectations that are unclear will lose energy and interest. When we give them the power to commit, they are more likely to engage in making something happen.

If You Use Them Improperly

Many people do not know how to construct a solid request, and leave out some of the elements critical to a successful outcome. Some people also accept promises even when they are not sure they can rely on them, so they spend time waiting or micromanaging other people. Unfortunately, what they are managing is usually not a performance agreement, but a people problem of some kind. Using Performance Conversations with all the elements of *What-When-Why* and *Who-Where-How* can reduce people problems by clarifying expectations and responsibilities.

Managing people by making demands is a short-term strategy. Demands without dialogue are acceptable in an emergency, but as a regular workplace practice, this can erode potentially productive relationships. Similarly, Performance Conversations that do not contain a timeline or do not address the availability of resources are likely to fail. The failure can lead to skepticism about the use of Performance Conversations, and result in not using them at all.

At some point, a manager must learn to have Performance Conversations (i.e., make good requests and get good promises). The Performance Conversation is a vehicle that gives people more say in their work, including work planning, scheduling, and processing, which supports them in being be more effective and more valuable. These conversations are so important to the culture of a group and the pace of progress on any initiative that it is worth developing mastery in using them.

If You Use Too Many Performance Conversations

Using too many Performance Conversations can produce an overload of work that people cannot complete, resulting in unfulfilled promises. Our informal research shows it takes an average of five to six separate actions, some of which can be very time consuming, to fulfill even a relatively simple promise. For example, one administrator promised to maintain a monthly status update for his board, which required sending, receiving, and reading multiple emails; reading reports and meeting with several people to obtain information; and preparing the status update report. If our estimate is accurate, anyone who has made ten promises will end up doing an average of fifty to sixty different things to complete them. At some point, the work required to keep the promises becomes overwhelming, and people experience work overload and the chronic sense of being behind.

Managing requests and promises requires three crucial skills: people need to know how to maintain a list of action items (a to-do list or a due list), keep a current calendar for scheduling appointments and deliverables, and use the calendar to schedule and perform the work required to prepare for them.

Anyone who trusts all their commitments to memory, or schedules only their appointments and due dates without also scheduling the time required to do the work, will need to improve their time and results management skills before they can make responsible promises or follow up on the promises of others.

If we overuse Performance Conversations before people have learned to respond responsibly, we can inundate them with expectations they cannot satisfy. Too many Performance Conversations will overload these skills and cause more problems than they cure.

Putting It into Practice

Practicing Performance Conversations will strengthen the skills needed to establish performance agreements with other people. It is a skill necessary for delegation and management. It also supports effective communication and honest relationships. A good place to practice having complete Performance Conversations is with someone with whom you already have a good working relationship. Practice making your next request using the following questions:

- Here is *What* I am asking you to do, *When* I want it, and *Why.*
- *Who* else do you think might be involved or included?
- Do you know
- *How* do you think you might accomplish this? Do you have a plan?

- Can you do this? Is there time in your schedule? Do you see anything that could prevent you from completing it?
- Do you accept my request?

Be prepared to make changes in your request based on their answers. You might even find it necessary to withdraw the request and ask someone else. As you gain experience, practice your Performance Conversations with more people, even the ones who do not report to you.

If you have any hesitation about having this kind of "straight-talk" Performance Conversation, remember that it helps other people more than it hurts. People want to know how to do what you want and need—even your bosses. People want to be clear about your expectations, and they welcome the chance to have a say in the performance agreements that help clarify and define them. You are helping people be successful in accomplishing something worthwhile. So practice.

To manage your own requests and promises, you can track them using a chart similar to the one below:

Table 7

What Did I Request or Promise?	When Is the Result Due?	Who Accepted the Request or Promise?	Do They Know Why It's Important?	Do They Know Where the Results Go and Resources Are Coming From?	Do They Know How the Job Will Get Done?
1					

What Did I Request or Promise?	When Is the Result Due?	Who Accepted the Request or Promise?	Do They Know Why It's Important?	Do They Know Where the Results Go and Resources Are Coming From?	Do They Know How the Job Will Get Done?
2					
3					

Chapter Five

Closure Conversations: Create Endings

When Ed Koch was mayor of New York, he was concerned about the number of accidents resulting from bikers darting in and out of traffic. Determined to solve the problem, he had "bike lanes"painted on the sides of city streets. But instead of making things better, the bike lanes actually made things worse. Drivers, undeterred by the double yellow lines identifying bike lanes, crossed them so frequently that police could not write enough tickets, and accidents involving bikers increased. As a result, Mayor Koch had the bike lanes removed, ending a futile exercise that cost the city millions of dollars.

Plenty of editorial space was given to criticizing the blunder and Koch's poor judgment. Reporters, looking for blood, sought interviews with the beleaguered mayor. In one television interview he agreed to, which was scheduled to last thirty minutes, the host was armed with a list of questions that were sure to make Koch look bad. The host began by asking, "Mayor Koch, you spent millions of taxpayer dollars to paint those bike lanes only to remove them. That tax money could have gone to valuable social services. What do you have to say for yourself?"

Pausing, Mayor Koch replied, "You're absolutely right. It was a huge mistake. I made the wrong decision, and I apologize."The host, stunned by the mayor's response, gathered herself and proceeded through her list of questions, each of which was an accusation of some kind. To each accusation, Mayor Koch gave a similar response, admitting the mistake and apologizing for it. The interview lasted for only five of the scheduled thirty minutes after which the topic was dropped, never to be raised again. [1]

Mayor Koch's success in this interview demonstrates the power of Closure Conversations. By acknowledging the facts that New Yorkers already knew—that the bike lanes were an idea that didn't work—and then apologizing for it, Mayor Koch completely disarmed the issue and brought it to a close. In the process, he restored some of the confidence that New Yorkers had lost in his stewardship of the city.

Closure Conversations can restore credibility and confidence, reduce resentment, build accomplishment and accountability, add velocity, and increase the engagement of participants and potential participants.

An Incomplete Past Can Prevent a New Future

The purpose of a Closure Conversation is to bring parts of the past to a conclusion, thus making room to start something new or to restart something that has become bogged down. Incomplete items such as tasks not done or communications not delivered at the end of a day, a week, or a project, can keep people stuck or prevent them from moving swiftly or confidently into their next actions. Closure Conversations acknowledge the facts, determine what will complete something that is unfinished, and allow people to move ahead.

The implementation of a new document tracking system in a city department was on hold for several months because no one was willing to make a decision. Should the department put out a request for proposals to get input from document management vendors? Or should staff members talk with officials in another department to see if they could develop a shared system? These two questions cycled back and forth, and eventually mushroomed into dozens of other, smaller questions. The document management committee worked to answer each one as it arose.

Rather than face the urgency of making a decision before the budget deadline, people on the committee held their meetings and discussed the same issues, asking and answering the same questions again and again. They were stuck in a struggle with familiar Understanding Conversations, and they were hoping some breakthrough idea would arise on its own. Everyone wanted to arrive at the decision by understanding all issues, and did not want to "put pressure on" the two senior people of the committee who would ultimately have to make the decision.

The committee eventually missed the budget deadline, disbanded its meetings, and the document tracking system was never implemented.

Incomplete items are a source of distress for many people, and can lead to distortions in our communications with others. Hans Christian Andersen's story

Laura had just completed a mandatory training period and was assigned to a new work section. She did not know that the people in the section she was joining had a reputation within the organization of being jokers because they liked to play pranks and make fun of each other. During an informal gathering around the copy machine, one of the regular employees played a practical joke on Laura; everyone laughed except Laura. Caught off guard and embarrassed, she did not know what to say or do, and, saying nothing, she returned to her cubicle feeling humiliated and ashamed. Because that sort of prank was standard practice among the section's employees, no one said anything to her, assuming she would get used to it.

Unfortunately, she did not. The event became the pea under the mattress in her relationship with her coworkers, and she was stuck with feeling embarrassed and unable to move beyond it. She made it a practice to stay away from informal gatherings and avoid the person who had played the joke on her. Soon the other employees accepted that Laura was a "loner, " which served to make her the target of more jokes and ridicule. After several weeks, Laura asked for a transfer to another section.

The Four A's of Closure Conversations

Closure conversations remove the peas from under mattresses by (a) recognizing that they are there, and (b) giving people an opportunity to say what will complete or eliminate them. Calling attention to something that is incomplete will bring it out into the open where people can see and discuss it, deal with it, and complete it.

Acknowledge the Facts: Say What's So

At the end of a project, while many things have been accomplished, usually others were either overlooked or left unresolved or not communicated. That is why some people can look at an obvious accomplishment and see only the errors or the miscommunications that happened along the way or the flaws in the end result. When we do not acknowledge these incomplete items, they can accumulate until the pace of work and communication slows down or, ultimately, stops progress altogether.

Charged with determining how to reduce infant mortality in a major metropolitan area, the Council on Infant Mortality started each meeting by reporting the latest infant mortality statistics from the health department. Over the previous several months, infant mortality had decreased slightly, so members were expecting a further decrease this month. However, when the health representative read the statistics, they learned that infant mortality had spiked upward. Rather than accept the statistics and look for what might have caused the undesirable outcome, council members challenged the data and argued among themselves about its validity.

"We were in denial, " the council chairperson said later. "We simply did not want to accept that infant mortality could have gone up that much in such a short period of time. Instead of moving forward with the rest of the agenda, we ended up arguing about the data. Was it collected properly? Who did the analysis? Did the data collectors count different neighborhoods this time?"

"If the health commissioner had not stepped into our meeting, we would probably still be at it. She listened, and each time we challenged the data, she would recognize the challenge and then bring us back to the factual statistic reported by the health department. She must have repeated that number ten times. Eventually we realized that none of our arguments were going to change the statistic."

Finally, the commissioner told the council members, "The statistic is what it is, and since you are committed to reducing infant mortality, I suggest you accept the data and get to work on what to do about it. You can't just accept the numbers when they are good and argue with them when they are bad."

The commissioner's Closure Conversation acknowledged the statistic for what it was, and helped the council members let go of their concerns about the data and return to their concerns about the causes of infant mortality. At that point, the dismal statistic became only a report on the current facts regarding infant mortality. Council members went back to work on what to do to bring the number back down.

Sometimes there is no hard data to acknowledge, as when people simply do not share the same point of view. One person believes he or she is right and the other is wrong. If they stick with the argument, they can never move forward to make progress.

That is when it is useful to acknowledge that the other person's point of view is valid, even when you do not agree with it. Let people know you hear them, instead of dismissing or arguing with what they are saying. This can create enough closure to get back into action. Using acknowledgment as a device for creating closure often eliminates the need for people to defend their point of view and keep the argument going.

Derek had a problem with Russell, a fellow manager in his department. Typically, they would argue over who should do certain jobs and how they should be done. Both were quick to point out the other's mistakes and find fault with the way the other did things, even when those ways were successful. Each defended his own actions while criticizing the other's.

Derek had been sharing an intern with Russell, and when Derek reassigned the intern to complete a project for his team, it made the intern unavailable to work for Russell at the same time. Russell was furious and called Derek, saying, "You had no right to reassign that intern without checking with me. How do you know I didn't have something as urgent or important as you did for the intern? Why do you think your needs are more important than mine?"

Derek told us, "Normally at this point, I would have defended myself and criticized him for something. I usually would give Russell an excuse or remind him of all the times he did things that affected me without checking. I did not do that this time."

"Instead, "Derek reported, "I told Russell, 'You know, you're right. I should have consulted with you before reassigning her. It was inconsiderate of me, and I apologize. I will release the intern until we have a chance to discuss it. How would that be?' That took Russell by surprise—he was quiet, and for a moment, I thought we were disconnected."

Then Russell said, "Thanks, but you don't have to do that. I'm sure you had a good reason, but I would appreciate if you'd talk to me about changes like that in the future."

Derek told us, "Since then we have not had as many arguments as before. We still disagree about things, but it is different now. There doesn't seem to be the same hostility."

Derek's communication was a break from a contentious way of relating that was gaining momentum between him and Russell, and it opened the door for a new way of communicating. He acknowledged that Russell's point of view was a valid one and offered to change his assignment for the intern. It took the fight out of their relationship and broke the habit of attacking and defending. Each of them now reports an increased willingness to collaborate and a new ability to hear what the other is saying.

Acknowledge persistent complaints and conditions. Another kind of fact to acknowledge is that every organization has a set of persistent complaints or subjects that people grouse about. Maybe it is about the managers, or the work environment, or certain policies or communication habits. One common habit may be that people say things like, "We have no leadership, " "Communication is poor, " or, "They don't tell us anything, but expect us to do everything." In some instances, the complaints persist year after year even when there is a high staff turnover—new staff members pick up the traditional organizational complaints very quickly. One manager invented a novel solution, without realizing that it was a form of Closure Conversation.

Erica was in charge of a customer service team that handled customer complaints, returns, and refunds at the back of a large retail store. She noticed when new staff members were hired, it took less than two months for them to start saying the usual gripes about working in customer complaints. Two things stood out. First, the staff got tired of hearing customer complaints all day, and said it was too negative to work there for very long. The staff's slogan was, "Customer service is really complaint headquarters." Second, the staff liked to say, "You can't pay people enough to put up with customers."

"People are quick to learn to complain about the customers, " Erica said. "One day, I posted a big blank signboard in our meeting room, where customers couldn't see it. At the top of the board, it said, "Cranky Customer Complaints." I handed staff members a stack of Post-its, and told them to make a note of every cranky customer they talked to, and write down the complaint. They laughed and didn't believe me, but I told them that I was serious. I wanted a closer look at the negative part of our job, and asked them to trust me and do it for a week."

"They started filling up that board fast! By the end of the week, there were over seventy notes posted. I took the notes home and summarized the results, which indicated that most of the customer complaints had to do with merchandise on the 'weekly sale' racks. We talked about this at the Monday meeting, and the employees had suggestions about how to prevent some of the complaints. They had never talked about solving the situation before, and even though our discussion sounded a lot like another gripe session, this time they were talking about how to fix a problem instead of being discouraged about something that could never be solved."

"I took their suggestions to the floor managers, and we had several meetings about my team's suggestions. Some changes have been made, and others are still going on. In the meantime, my staff members are not the same: they don't complain about customers so much. We are keeping the Cranky Customer board going so we can keep learning. It is much nicer to work here now than it has ever been, and staff turnover has dropped a lot."

Workplace complaints can become part of a background understanding where people talk as if some undesirable conditions are unchangeable. A conversation that recognizes the existence of a persistent complaint or difficult situation brings it out of the background and makes it visible. This can bring closure simply by having people look more closely, get more specific, and break up the habitual pattern of complaints.

Appreciate the People: Recognize Accomplishment and Contribution

Research shows that many people feel underappreciated and under-recognized at work. Gallup, for example, reports that less than one-third of employees can say that, "In the last seven days, I have received recognition or praise for doing good work."[2]

When we ask managers, "How many of you are confident that what you do really matters or makes a difference to your organization?" only a few hands go up. When we ask, "How many of you feel fully recognized, acknowledged, and appreciated for the work you do?" even fewer hands go up. Finally, when we ask, "How many of you make sure the people who do things for you would say that *they*feel fully recognized, acknowledged, and appreciated for what they do?" almost no hands go up. Is it any wonder that only 30% of nonmanagers, 40% of managers, and 50% of executives report being fully engaged in their work?[3]

It is tempting to blame lack of engagement on such things as poorly designed incentive plans or overly sensitive people. Unfortunately, that puts the problem of disengaged people on things beyond our control. If we want people to be more engaged in their work—which will improve productivity, performance, and relationships—we can learn to use appreciative Closure Conversations.

Appreciating people is an easy and inexpensive Closure Conversation, and it can restore even cynical people to a more active level of participation in their work. Words of appreciation can shift an interaction out of an unproductive rut and give attention to people's positive behaviors and accomplishments. People respond to positive reinforcement in all aspects of life. When we recognize others for good work, or for being cooperative and thoughtful, we encourage them to continue being that way.

Scott was in charge of developing a new promotion strategy for a well-established product his client wanted to reposition in the market. The client told Scott he wanted a radical, "out-of-the-box" type of approach. Scott worked with his most creative associates and came up with an innovative and contemporary set of ideas. Unfortunately, when the client saw it, he got cold feet and scrapped the whole campaign. Disappointed, Scott met with his boss to let him know what happened. To his surprise, his boss did not focus on the failure, but on what had been accomplished.

His boss said, "Scott, I know the loss of the campaign is a personal disappointment to you, and I'm confident you will look to see what we can learn from losing the contract for it. But don't lose sight of what you accomplished in doing the preparation for the proposal. The approach you developed is unlike any we have tried before. It combines media and technologies in a creative way, and it has many ideas we could use in campaigns for other clients. Did you fail to get the contract? Yes, but you also produced something that will be valuable going forward. I want to thank you for the extraordinary work you did."

People do not like to fail, and they usually work hard to avoid it. Scott's boss knew he would be unhappy about the failure and that it would preoccupy his thinking, perhaps costing his productivity and participation in upcoming projects.

He acknowledged the facts—that Scott had failed and was disappointed—and then set about appreciating the accomplishments and the value. Scott did not dwell long on the failure, and shared the praise with his associates, getting everyone back to work with new energy and enthusiasm.

Giving recognition can be more powerful than giving reprimands. We often hear managers complain that they want their people to demonstrate more initiative. Those same managers often forget to thank or praise people who show initiative, such as by sharing new ideas, shortcuts, or ways to improve products or services. The more we let people know when they do something right, the more we reinforce their good behaviors. And, according to Cindy Ventrice, author of *Make Their Day!,* recognizing people for what they accomplish is in our own self-interest because it can end up making our job easier.[4]

Marshall was a daytime supervisor in a factory with twenty-four-hour services. He was having problems with a maintenance supervisor from the night shift.

"This guy really hates me, " Marshall said. "We only ever speak through email, but his emails are nasty. He uses profanity and says some really mean things. I now don't answer his emails until it is convenient for me. Then, when I do send him an email, it just says, "Done." He probably doesn't like the way I interact with him, but who needs that kind of abuse?"

Marshall learned about Closure Conversations and decided to try an experiment with the troubling maintenance supervisor. He planned a different way of responding the next time he got one of the "nasty-grams." Within a week, he had his opportunity. He received an unfriendly message that accused him of botching a machine maintenance job that hadn't been finished properly. Marshall was determined to test the Closure Conversation idea.

"Instead of ignoring the email, " he said, "I replied immediately, and I told him, 'Sorry John, I am stuck in a production application problem here and will get back to you in half an hour.' Then, as soon as I could, I gave him a response about the machine maintenance situation. I didn't hear anything back, but the next morning, at the end of his shift, he came to my office. I was amazed because he had never done that before. Then he asked me for assistance on a procedure his crew was having difficulty getting right."

"I was shocked, " Marshall said. "Maybe he liked the fast response, or that my email said more than, 'Done.' Whatever it was, that one conversation seemed to change things for us. It actually felt good to help him out with the procedure issues he was having and help get everything to work out for him and his crew. Now I feel better toward him, and I don't get nasty emails anymore either. All this from one conversation!"

"Since then, I make it a point to respond when people email me a question or some information. I send an email back saying, 'Thank you, ' or, 'I will get back to you later this morning.' This closure idea has changed the way I work and the way people talk to me."

Apologize for Mistakes and Misunderstandings

Everyone makes mistakes. Sometimes we overstep boundaries or violate accepted principles or norms. We forget to do the things we promised, creating problems for other people and ourselves. Sometimes we do things we think will be helpful or appropriate, only to find out that others see things differently. A few examples:

Jonathan made the mistake of speaking out of turn and interrupting a senior manager at an executive meeting; everyone got quiet and looked disapprovingly at him. Jonathan did not speak again for the rest of the meeting.

Rob, a software developer, promised his team he would complete a crucial section of code by the following morning. Then he got distracted with another project, and the code was never written. He and his team had to stay late the next day to complete the job.

Sharon, a management consultant, told everyone at a meeting of her client's managers that she would take the information she had collected on a particular issue and pull it together into a report for the group to review. After the meeting, Sharon learned that one of the senior managers was upset because he thought she was intruding on his authority. He felt threatened by her promise to produce a report, and withdrew his support for her consulting work.

In each case, an interpersonal issue intruded on a potentially productive discussion, and it could have been defused by an apology or a personal conversation. Mayor Koch showed the way: a public admission of his mistake in building bike lanes in New York ended a controversy that had enveloped City Hall. It takes courage to admit a mistake and apologize for having caused inconvenience or distress for other people. We fear that an apology can make us look weak or incompetent, damage our reputation or career, be used as ammunition against us, or embarrass us and cause a loss of respect and credibility in the eyes of others.[5]

Mayor Koch probably had the same concerns, but he also knew and trusted the power of telling the truth. He could have blamed New York drivers for not obeying the law, or city planners for not anticipating the problem. But he didn't, and his openness and honesty improved people's perception of him as a good leader. Research shows that honesty is the one characteristic most admired and looked for in leaders.[6]

An apology is a form of Closure Conversation, and, oddly enough, it can be useful even when you are not sure whether you made a mistake or not. One manager we know says his motto is, "Apologize even when it's not your fault." We shared this with an MBA student who was having problems with a team member, and he decided to test the idea.

Doug said, "Ever since I joined my current project team about a year ago, I have had issues with one guy who had been with the group for over five years. Unfortunately, he was supposed to be a mentor for me, but from the very beginning, it seemed like he just had it in for me. He was sarcastic to me in front of others, excluded me from meetings, and never seemed like he took the job of mentoring me too seriously. For the life of me, I could not figure out what he had against me, especially since I knew I hadn't done anything to him."

"I swallowed my pride and decided to apologize to him for somehow causing him a problem. I waited until Friday afternoon, in case things didn't go smoothly, walked into his cubicle, and asked if he had a minute."

"I began apologizing for whatever it was I may have done to upset him. I felt like I was rambling, which I probably was, because he was not saying anything in return. I felt more awkward as he continued to just sit, listen, and say nothing. I finally concluded by saying that I hoped he could put whatever I did behind him so we could maintain a good work relationship."

"All he said was, 'I guess.' I felt like a fool as I walked back to my desk, digesting what had just transpired. I was disappointed with his lack of response. I thought he would say more than 'I guess, ' and I started to question whether I handled the conversation correctly."

"To my surprise, about two hours later, I got an email from him. He said I had done nothing to him, but that my apology made him reconsider the way he was behaving toward me. He said even though he was supposed to be mentoring me, he actually viewed me as a threat, thinking that I might 'steal some of his thunder.' He ended by saying we were on good terms and that he would like for us to start over so we could work together cooperatively in the future."

"I am amazed at this. I had no idea that apologizing for something I didn't do could have this kind of impact. It got him thinking, and the result was it cleared the air. My whole work experience has changed for the better."

We have seen many examples of Closure Conversations similar to Doug's. When people feel wronged or threatened, they often do not know how to communicate in a way that lets go of their negative experience. Instead, they change their behavior to a "fight or flight" response. Doug's mentor took the "fight" response and became difficult and confrontational. Others take the "flight" response and withdraw from subsequent interactions.

In either case, the result is that people withhold their performance to make others pay for their transgressions and wrongdoings, whether they actually happened or not. A well-handled apology is an easy solution to breaking up this knot, and, because it is such an extraordinary thing to do, it provides a way to address a personal problem without making anyone defensive.

Attorneys once told doctors not to apologize when bad things happened to their patients, but now those attorneys are changing their advice. They once feared an apology was an admission of fault that could result in losing a malpractice suit. In 2001, the University of Michigan Health System dropped the traditional "deny and defend" approach in favor of honest disclosure and apology. Over the subsequent five years, the number of active malpractice cases, along with the time and cost to resolve them, dropped dramatically.

Apparently, the top motivating factor for malpractice lawsuits was the patient's anger, which was only made worse by the doctor's silence and denial. By the end of 2007, twenty-nine states had passed laws that prevent doctors' expressions of sympathy and condolence from being used against them in court. Hospitals and malpractice insurance companies are now telling doctors to have open and honest discussions with their patients. They are even teaching doctors how to apologize correctly.[7]

Amend Broken Agreements: The Four R's

The "broken windows" theory says that a single broken window left unrepaired in a building will signal a lax attitude toward the care and upkeep of property. Soon, other windows in the building will be broken, and other signs of deterioration will begin to appear around the building: accumulation of trash, graffiti, abandoned cars, and other junk. Eventually, as the neglect becomes obvious, other forms of crime such as panhandling, prostitution, and drug dealing take place in or near the building. People who live in the area start to feel vulnerable, and they either leave or avoid the area. The neighborhood deteriorates further and crime increases.[8]

Rudy Guiliani, then mayor of New York, and his chief of police William Bratton, believed in the "broken windows" theory enough to put it into action. They aggressively pursued graffiti artists, panhandlers, loiterers, subway turnstile jumpers, and other low-level crimes. They made the homeless stay in shelters, removed graffiti within twenty-four hours, and repaired broken windows in abandoned buildings. Although there was a lot of dissention about going after petty criminals, the result was that violent crimes declined by over 56% and property crimes by almost 65% during Guiliani's administration.[9]

Broken agreements are like broken windows. When people break an agreement to complete a job by a particular date, do quality work, or communicate honestly, it sends two signals. First, it says that particular agreement is not important. Second, it says keeping agreements in general is not important. If one broken agreement goes unacknowledged, more will be broken as people realize that keeping promises does not matter much even when threatened with legal sanction.[10] At that point, a culture of cynicism and uncertainty is gaining ground.

When agreements are broken, as they surely will be, a Closure Conversation can help to restore trust in the relationship. There are four steps—the Four R's—to address and repair broken agreements, which will build and strengthen accountability in much the same way that repairing broken windows improves a neighborhood.

Step 1.

Step 2. **Report.** Both parties meet and communicate about the fact that an agreement has been broken, what the agreement was, and what exactly did or did not happen. Reporting is an acknowledgement type of Closure Conversation and needs to include mention of any costs or consequences resulting from the broken promise. Ideally, both parties will see where they fell short and take ownership of their respective roles, but this does not always happen.

Step 3. **Repair.** Both parties, having recognized the costs of the broken agreement, ask, "What will make this right?" The repair needs to be spelled out in a way that both parties are clear about the actions, results, and timelines that are appropriate to clean up the breakage.

Step 4. **Recommit.** The damage has been done, identified, and communicated. A new agreement has been made to repair the damage. The final step is to restore the relationship by agreeing to honor promises in a new way in the future. Prevent damage to the future of the relationship by agreeing that a new future starts now.

Amending broken agreements is an ongoing part of managing the accomplishment of even the smallest task or project. It lets people know that talk is not cheap and that their word matters. It also clears the air of a great deal of the guilt or defensiveness that can become a barrier to individual productivity and group creativity.

The "Four A's"—Acknowledge the facts, Appreciate the people, Apologize for mistakes and misunderstandings, and Amend broken agreements—can be used independently or in combinations. There are times when all that is needed is an acknowledgement of the facts to let people know the status of things. At other times, appreciation is sufficient to restore people, or an apology or amended agreement is enough to clear the air so that people can return their attention to the job at hand. But we know many people who make it a point to use all four A's in each Closure Conversation to be sure that they defuse every aspect of a difficult (or potentially difficult) situation.

Build Accountability and Resolve "People Problems"

"We need people to be more accountable" is a popular wish of many managers. Unfortunately, they often talk about accountability as if it is a personality trait, an attitude, or some characteristic of an individual person. In fact, accountability is a product of conversations between two or more people. Accountability is an aspect of a relationship, not of an individual, and you can build and strengthen it with Closure Conversations.

According to Merriam Webster, accountability is a willingness to account for one's actions. As ASTD's research shows, people are most likely to do a task when they know they will have to account for it. An accountability conversation, in which people account for their actions and results, is a special form of Closure Conversation. It is sometimes called a status report, a debrief conversation, an after-action review, or a postmortem, in which participants report on the status of tasks and results, examine breakdowns and breakthroughs in order to learn what worked and what didn't, and adjust future plans and timelines accordingly.

An accountability conversation is an application of the first type of Closure Conversation: Acknowledge the facts. This can also be seen as a feedback conversation, and ideally, it is built into every task assignment and project schedule. Giving each assignment a regular status report schedule is a way to strengthen accountability by ensuring that there will be a conversation to account for whatever happened in the process of doing the job. When the factual results are good, or better than expected, you can add in a Closure Conversation to appreciate the people. When the results are not good, you have the opportunity to strengthen accountability in several ways.

If the Result Doesn't Meet Expectations

Sometimes people fail to deliver what they promised: the structure is wrong, something is missing or inaccurate, or the quality of work is low in some other way. Making clear requests for what you want, explaining why it is important, and getting good promises from people will all help reduce the frequency of quality problems.

Harry is a processing plant manager. Pete, an engineer, promised Harry he would research a new compressor to see if it would improve one of the plant's process measures. Harry specified he wanted a report that included specific information and a table of comparisons. Pete delivered the report, but he omitted putting in the table of comparisons. That meant Harry had to have a Closure Conversation to let Pete know that parts of the promised result were missing, incomplete, or unacceptable. Harry called Pete to his office.

"Hey, Pete, thanks for coming by."

"Sure thing. You wanted to talk about the compressor specs I gave you?"

"I do. As I recall, one of the things you were going to do was put the comparisons in a table, but I don't see a table. What happened with that?"

"Ah, well, I thought the listings I gave you made the table unnecessary, so I didn't think it was needed."

"Yes, I can see what you mean, but I wish you had checked with me first. I intended to give the VP that table as a summary without sending her the full report. Now I can't do that without creating the table myself or asking you to redo it."

"I'm really sorry. It wouldn't have taken much to prepare the table; I just didn't think it was necessary. I have everything on the computer, so I can prepare it in no time."

"That would be very helpful. How soon can you do that?"

"About thirty minutes."

"Great, email it to me. That way I can forward it to the VP."

"Will do."

"One last thing. I just realized I didn't tell you why I wanted that table when we made our agreement."

"No, you said you wanted it, but you didn't say it was for the VP."

"That is my mistake, and I apologize for not telling you that I wanted the table to hand over to someone else. If I had done that, we wouldn't be having this meeting right now."

"True. But if I had done what you asked for, we wouldn't be meeting either. Instead of making assumptions about what you needed, I should have checked with you. I guess we both learned something."

"Looks like it. I'll look for your email in about thirty minutes."

"It'll be there."

When It's Late

Making good requests and promises improves accountability, especially if everyone involved agrees to a specific due date. A few tips on building accountability for timelines are:

- Follow up immediately after the deadline has occurred. Whether you receive the result at the agreed time or not, a prompt follow-up is a way of communicating that the deadline matters and that you care about it.

- When the people you are working with have little experience in being accountable, don't wait until the deadline—have a reminder conversation with them prior to the deadline. This lets people know the promise is still alive and your expectations are too.

In the case of Harry and Pete, they had a good working relationship going back more than two years. Harry knew Pete took their agreements seriously, but if Pete was ever even a little bit late, Harry knew he needed to communicate quickly. He also knew he had to continue being specific about the time requirements when he talked to Pete.

"Hey, Pete, this is Harry."

"Hi, Harry. What's up?"

"I am following up on that table you were going to send me. I know it has only been forty-five minutes, but I want to be sure you didn't forget about it."

"Ouch, I got distracted on the way back to my office. One of the maintenance guys stopped me with a problem on repairing a seal on the valves. I'm working on your table now, though, and it is just about done. I can have it for you in ten more minutes. Will that be OK?"

"OK, but the VP is leaving today at 3:30 PM, and I need to get it to her before that."

"For sure you will have it in ten minutes. I'll email it to you, and I'll call you to confirm it's on the way."

"Thanks, I appreciate it."

Don't Let People off the Hook

People learn that our requests and promises matter when we follow up with them. Depending on the capability and experience of the people with whom you make agreements, you may need to follow up only at the time the promise is due, or you may need to check in on them several times during the process of their fulfilling the promise.

We know one manager who swears by her method of making a "resource check" at the 25% mark on the timeline of every promise she makes with her supervisors and project managers. "By the time they are 25% of the way into the work, " she says, "they know more about the reality of their plan and the resources they really need. My resource check is something I now build into the schedule of every timeline. We review the staff levels assigned to the project, the equipment and supplies, the vendor agreements, and anything else that could alter the timeline."

She says her resource check accomplishes two things. First, it allows for an adjustment of resources after people have started a project and learned more about what they really need. Second, it is a reminder that the promise and the timeline are important.

Managers who do not use a resource check or status debrief partway through their assignments can expect some failures in quality or timeliness.

With failures, come excuses. If you accept people's excuses for failures of quality or time, you do a disservice to their future performance as individuals and as a group. This does not mean anyone needs to be scolded or punished. It does require a Closure Conversation that reviews and acknowledges the facts and itemizes where things went off track. Whenever we let people get by without that conversation, we undermine their ability to be accountable as well as undermining our own credibility in managing agreements with people.

"I've been with this company for twenty-three years, " Duane said. "I've had six bosses in that time. None of them have ever been serious about what they say they want. When I started here, a supervisor told me that he never did anything unless the boss asked him for something two times. He said he used to do things right away, but then he found out the person who asked for it had changed his mind, forgotten about it, or wanted something different. So he made it his policy to wait until he received a second request, figuring that if someone asked about it again, he or she was probably serious.

"Over the years I have been here, I think my supervisor gave me pretty good advice. All my bosses ask me for things, and then they forget about them and never get back to me. It's not that I'm lazy, but I don't want to waste my time on things that nobody cares about."

If you want people to honor their promises with you, it is important to honor your promises with them by following up on or before the due date. The failure to follow through with Closure Conversations can be a manager's own worst enemy when it comes to building a culture of accountability.

It is also important, as part of improving accountability, to take responsibility for the rebuilding part of a Closure Conversation. When a manager has identified a problem, he or she is obligated to bring it to light and look for a way to address it in a way that it will not recur.

"Hey, Pete, this is Harry."

"Hi, Harry. What's up?"

"I got the table you sent me, and I've passed it along to the VP. Thanks."

"No problem."

"One other thing, though. I want you to know I would like to ratchet up the way we make agreements. I sometimes think I am doing a little too much micromanaging with you, because you are pulled in so many directions that you wind up being late on some of the things you promise me. You've got me trained to call you and remind you about things, and to check up on you more than I like. Any suggestions about how we could change that?"

"Oh, wow. I see what you mean. I never realized that my way of working was causing you to do more work. Let me think about that, and what I could do. Come to think of it, I could probably start by clearing some of the stacks off my desk, and start using my calendar to track what I'm promising."

"Sounds like a good start. I may bring this up again, but I appreciate your looking for ways to be more time sensitive."

"Thanks. Talk tomorrow."

Defuse Resentment and Upsets

During the America Cup races, boats are taken out of the water every night and their hulls scrubbed and polished in order to remove barnacles, roughness, or protrusions that could increase turbulence and surface drag. Keeping the hulls clean allows the boats greater speed and more accurate maneuverability. What if there was a way to remove the barnacles that impair management and productive relationships in the workplace?

People who are resentful or upset about something, or who are working with people who are upset, will not be able to work at their full potential. People's upsets are like the flu: they are distracting for the people who have them and can infect the people who are nearby, pulling attention away from work and onto the details and moods of the distressed person.

Resentments and other upsets are like barnacles impeding workplace performance—they slow things down.

It happens every day: someone says or does something to somebody else, and suddenly someone's reaction becomes a barnacle of resentment, irritation, or worry. Unfortunately, we cannot take our workplace interactions out of the water every night and scrape them off to start fresh tomorrow with clean communication. Closure Conversations are the tools we can use to dissolve workplace barnacles, and they can dissolve even very old ones.

George, the new manager of a vehicle service organization, planned to upgrade his maintenance team's technology by installing GIS and computer communication systems. He had already met with the fleet and service supervisors in one-on-one meetings, but planned to talk to the employees in both groups about scheduling the GIS installation and the training program that would bring everyone up to speed.

The discussion about the installation schedule went well, but when he handed out the training schedule, several employees seemed angry, saying, "This isn't going to be fair for the back room machine guys, ""You're going around us again, " and "This won't work any better than it did last time." Since he knew from previous conversations that they all wanted the

GIS system, he was caught off guard by this resistance.

After listening, George said, "The training will help you use the system that you all agree you want. What is going on? Really, I want to know what this is about."

After a moment of hesitation, one fleet employee said, "The manager who was here before you told us we had to attend trainings for a new purchasing and inventory system. He said if we did the training, we'd get promotions and pay raises."

"Yes, " another mechanic said. "He said if we could switch over to a new purchasing system in eight weeks, we'd get promoted. So we did it. We got the training, and then we transferred all our inventory data, and updated the inventory records and reports. We did it in less than eight weeks."

Their previous manager, however, was ultimately unable to obtain the promotions or the raises for the employees. He never had a Closure Conversation with the supervisors. Instead, he tried to cover it up by making other adjustments. He permitted three of four supervisors to receive overtime opportunities that boosted their income. The fourth man had not been with the company long enough to be classified in a way that made him eligible for overtime, so the manager gave him a special title and promised a change when he reached his two-year anniversary. By the time the anniversary date came, the manager had left the company. Although the men could never prove it, they believed their manager never intended to obtain the raises and promotions. Further, they had convinced themselves that his decisions had racial and cultural overtones. Their resentment had only hardened since that time.

George realized that, whatever the truth, some of his employees believed they had been betrayed. All it took was the word "training, " and it brought back all the grudges of that past incident. George knew he had not been the cause of the problem, but he also knew he was going to live with its consequences until he found a way to resolve it. He chose to take the broken agreement approach. He acknowledged the agreement his predecessor had made, recognized that it had not been kept, and offered his genuine apology, on behalf of the company.

"You were misled, " he told them. "The way it was handled showed a lack of respect for you and the work you do. I want to personally apologize to each one of you. And I will look into this to see what I can to do make it right.

George met with the human resources director and the operations vice president, and followed through to see that his employees were properly classified and received the best increases available in the budget. Three weeks later, the human resources director came to meet personally with the supervisors to tell them when the new pay scale would begin. Their skepticism finally dissolving, one inventory supervisor said, "It's great to get this squared away, but you know what made the biggest difference to me? Seeing that George was shocked and sorry to find out we had been treated like that in the first place. The way he said he was sorry, even though he hadn't done anything, I knew we had a friend."

George said later, "I think the previous manager did the best he could at the time. I probably would not have been able to do any better than he did, but he made a mistake in not following through to get their pay raises the following year. I wonder if I would have been honest enough to apologize for that incident if it had been me who caused it in the first place. I'd like to think so."

By dealing with the broken promise on its own merits, George not only completed something his predecessor left incomplete, but also enhanced his credibility and earned the respect of his men. It would have been very easy for him to dismiss their complaints as "just resistance, " but he listened well and was able to strengthen his relationship with his staff. His experience is a reminder that the velocity we experience during a project may have little or nothing to do with the current plan. However old the barnacles are, a Closure Conversation can help people let go and get back to work.

If You Are Missing Closure Conversations

Closure Conversations are commonly used, but often we do not realize that they can be instruments to accelerate performance. We acknowledge the facts of the matter when a situation demands we do it, but we can also acknowledge the "what's so" facts of a situation as a device for getting unstuck. Similarly, we can learn to recognize accomplishments and mistakes as a reliable way to keep people engaged and doing their best, or to restore their spirit after a problem or breakdown in performance. We can give people better feedback, revitalize communications, and clean up past misunderstandings to develop a culture for strengthening accountability.

Closure Conversations touch every element of performance (i.e., the

If You Don't Use Closure Conversations

Many people do not use Closure Conversations, believing that they are unnecessary. This is the optimistic view that people will remember what they have committed to do, and will manage themselves, their resources, and their communications successfully. It is a failure of management to turn over responsibility for agreements to others without followthrough. Agreements are, after all, a two-way process of requests and promises, and thus deserve to be owned on both sides rather than handed off and never revisited.

Some people do not use Closure Conversations because they think they are either too personal or too confrontational. Appreciating accomplishment, for example, can be warm and supportive, which may be uncomfortable for someone who wants to maintain more workplace distance between people. Similarly, acknowledging someone's mistakes can be seen as punishing them, which could be uncomfortable for people who would rather be liked than respected.

Without Closure Conversations, however, a project can lose momentum, a workplace can acquire long-lasting baggage that compromises performance, and an entire organization can develop a culture of resignation and indifference. Managers who learn and practice using Closure Conversations will see a shift in the trust and credibility of workplace relationships, and communications will begin to become more reliable and productive.

If You Use Them Improperly

The primary misuse of Closure Conversations is a failure to listen to the people who are working on fulfilling their promises and agreements. When we cannot, or will not, hear what they are saying, they are left stuck with something they need to communicate. This undelivered communication can reduce their productivity and manageability in future communications.

When you pay attention to incomplete items, you set the tone that nothing is to be overlooked in either reaching for a goal or supporting people who are working on achieving one. Ask for, and act on, feedback and you will keep workplace communications focused on the desired results. It also helps when you must introduce course-corrections if plans need to change midstream. Closure Conversations are a time-tested way to accelerate changes small and large, and to gain people's involvement and interest in any endeavor.

If You Use Too Many Closure Conversations

As long as your Closure Conversations are well grounded in a commitment to creating or accomplishing something, they probably cannot be over-used. However, there can be an overdose of Closure Conversations when we lose sight of the initiatives we are looking to fulfill, or when our conversations are inauthentic. Debriefing people without reference to the original plan of action, for example, loses the reason we are involved in the project in the first place. Without this context, people can shift into busy mode, adding more anxiety and urgency, but without a sense of the purpose and value of their work. Similarly, if we are insincere in our appreciation or our apologies, people are likely to see us as patronizing and disingenuous, which will undermine our credibility and their trust in us.

Closure Conversations are useful to keep things moving and to support people in being responsible, accountable, and in communication with others. When you tie them to a larger goal or purpose and communicate honestly, they will deliver those benefits to the entire workplace.

Putting It into Practice

Closure Conversations return people to the purpose of their work, and support them in operating consistently with workplace intentions and initiatives. Sometimes they are personal conversations to support individuals and groups in joining (or returning to) the original proposal to make something new happen. But many Closure Conversations are impersonal, such as the display of a workplace scoreboard to show how many deals have been closed, services delivered, or timelines met. The idea is to manage the agreements between people and to support them in honoring their word.

People who want performance from others must master the Closure Conversation. The easiest way to begin is by acknowledging facts. Let people know, "I got it, " when they deliver things you asked for, so they do not wonder about it. Let people know, "Here's what happened, " when you learn something about events or communications that are relevant to their assignments.

Adding appreciation, even a simple, but sincere "thank you, " can make a difference in the way people respond to future requests. Apologies are sometimes harder, but when you catch yourself doing something that doesn't work, acknowledge it and apologize. It sets a tone that mistakes are not the end of the world.

One reason people fail to follow up on requests and promises is that they do not have a way to keep track of them. If you track your requests and promises using the table at the end of Chapter 4, you will be able to acknowledge the facts of work in progress and have status reviews at any time. This mechanism also allows you to have the Closure Conversations to follow up with people, and to amend agreements as needed.

A quick way to do this is to use a device some managers have tested (see the table below). If you maintain a list of each important project or initiative, (in rows), you can check at every meeting whether there is something that needs to be Acknowledged, Appreciated, Apologized for, or Amended. We know a few managers who have posted this table in their conference areas, and who invite their staffs to use it as a tool to identify what they need to address to increase velocity.

List of Initiative, Projects, or Tasks

	What Facts Do We Need to Acknowledge?	What People Do We Need to Appreciate, and For What?	What Mistakes or Misunder-standings Do We Need to Apologize For?	What Agreements Need to be Amended?
1				
2				
3				

Table 8

Finally, a Closure Conversation with respect to the entire initiative will complete the original intention and allow participants to debrief for the entire undertaking just as they do for individual requests and promises, and will make space for new initiatives. The table describing the initiative shown at the end of Chapter 3 is the product of Understanding Conversations, which means it contains the benefits of participant ideas and perspectives. We know managers who keep that version on their conference room wall. It helps everyone make updates as things change, so that everyone can see where things stand. It is also useful as a tool for remembering all the Closure Conversations that will be needed at the end of the project.

Chapter Six

Using the Four Conversations

When you learn to use the four types of conversations, you can put them to work in your work and life—especially in those areas where you want more success or fewer problems. When you know your own conversational tendencies, you can learn to develop your ability to use whichever conversations you need the most. You will then be able to put all four types of conversations together to address the specific situations that limit your success.

Conversational Tendencies

People use all four conversations, but with different levels of awareness and expertise. Most people tend to favor some conversations and under-use others. Unfortunately, we cannot get everything done with one or two conversations: we need all four.

Initiative: The Least Used Conversation

Initiatives are the least used of the four conversations because most of us are engaged in accomplishing goals and objectives that someone else has already initiated. Although we come up with good ideas every now and then, we generally do not push them forward as initiatives. The benefit of learning to have Initiative Conversations more often is that they are the source of innovation and change, and they open new paths for accomplishing things. You can practice Initiative Conversations by proposing your favorite ideas for actions and results in every area of your life.

Understanding: The Most Over-Used Conversation

People use Understanding Conversations more often than any other type of conversation. This often-excessive use stems from our persistent belief that people will take action when they understand what needs to be done. While this might happen sometimes, it is not the rule. As a result, we spend too much time explaining, describing, and answering questions instead of moving on to make a clear request for an action or outcome. You can practice using Understanding Conversations in new ways by testing some of the ideas in Chapter 3. Learning to move into Performance and Closure Conversations will also help reduce dependence on, and overuse of, Understanding Conversations.

Performance: The Least Developed Conversation

People use Performance Conversations, but not enough of them, and do not always include all the elements discussed in Chapter 4. Since Performance Conversations are the only ones that actually commit people to action, they are critical in determining the results you get. The way to live up to the cliché, "Work smarter, not harder, " is to use clear requests and promises. Performance Conversations can help you increase the reliability, quality, quantity, and timeliness of the results you want

Closure: The Most Neglected Conversation

Overall, there should be more Closure Conversations than Performance Conversations because, in addition to acknowledgement, appreciation, and apology, every request, promise, and initiative should have a Closure Conversation when it is completed—either to amend the agreement or to complete it in some other way.

Most organizations have Closure Conversations that acknowledge the facts of performance with status reports, project debriefs, and performance reviews as part of their established procedures. Unfortunately, most are missing the day-to-day Closure Conversations that acknowledge the status of requests and promises, express appreciation, and apologize for misunderstandings. Similarly, people often omit the conversations to amend agreements and update their requests and promises for results.

All of these types of Closure Conversations support trust, credibility, and accountability, and they strengthen people's engagement at work, increase creativity and new ideas, and build productivity. You can practice Closure Conversations by simply adding appreciation and apology to your repertoire, but you will get the greatest gains when you track your requests and promises, and follow up by acknowledging the facts of performance and amending the agreements for actions and outcomes.

How the Four Conversations Work Together

Although we have presented the four conversations in a linear fashion—Initiative, Understanding, Performance, and Closure—that is not necessarily the best sequence to produce the results you want. Sometimes, when you are launching new projects or changes, a linear sequence of the four conversations will be fine. Most likely, however, you will use them in different orders and combinations, depending on the situation and the results you want to accomplish.

For example, in the process of having a Closure Conversation, you may discover that new actions or results are needed, so you may choose to have a

Performance Conversation and make new requests and promises. In a second situation, a Closure Conversation may reveal new opportunities that you had not previously considered, so you can have an Initiative Conversation to get something new started. In a third situation Closure Conversation, you may learn that people are confused or uncertain about the intended outcomes, indicating the need for an Understanding Conversation.

There is no ideal or set pattern for the sequence or combination of the four conversations: the way you use them will depend on the success of your interactions. The decisive test of any conversational pattern is whether it is producing the desired results. If people seem to be busy, but you are not seeing the results you expected, look to your conversations. Which one are you missing? Are there any

If you confront any of the six limitations identified in Chapter 1, you have an opportunity to alter your conversational pattern and practice your conversational skills. You could:

- Have a Closure Conversation: Declare a breakdown, acknowledge that things are not working as expected, and find out what is clogging performance.
- Revisit your Performance Conversations: Clean up the requests and promises to make them more specific in every element.

- Have a new Understanding Conversation: Hold a Q&A session to find out what people don't understand.
- Have an Initiative Conversation to refresh the initiative and remind people of why their work matters.

The following review of the six limitations offers ideas on how to use the four conversations that you can test and customize to the needs of your situation.

Improve Other People's Performance

All managers, and many workers at all levels, have to get things done with, or through, other people. If some people are consistently late in getting things to you, or do not meet your quality standards, it can be frustrating and affect the other people around you. The most frequent responses to this kind of performance problem are:

1. Put up with it and hope they will do better next time
2. Explain how important it is to do quality on-time work, and hope they will be motivated (or feel obligated) to do better
3. Find a way to work around them by developing alternative resources, giving false early deadlines to avoid failure, or assign more of the work to others, including yourself

These solutions are weak because they do not develop people to get better at delivering good results. There is a better way: use Understanding, Performance, and Closure Conversations.

Reduce lateness. A group of 25 managers in a variety of organizations shared a similar complaint about late work: "People are not consistent in getting things to me on time." To determine the extent of the problem, each manager kept a record of all the promises people made for on-time work, and noted how many of the promises were met on time. These managers captured data for three weeks, and discovered the average reliability of promises kept was 56%. Then they experimented with different types of conversations and found that reliable on-time performance was a product of how well they combined three conversations: Understanding, Performance, and Closure.

First, Understanding. To have other people give you ontime results, you need to help them understand all the basic elements of performance (i.e., the *What-When-Why* and the *Who-Where-How*):

- *What* should the finished product or outcome look like?
- *When* do you want it?
- *Why* is this important?
- *Who* else is involved that they might need to talk with?
- *Where* should they go to get everything they need?
- Are there any useful tips on *How* to do the job?

Sometimes we expect people to figure all this out on their own, but if you are trying to improve someone's reliability, start by being generous and telling the person everything he or she needs to know.

Then, for your Performance Conversation, make a good, clear request: "I request X by this due date, subject to these conditions and specifications." Get a good promise in return: confirm that the person knows *What* you want and *When,* that he or she is available for doing the work, and will obtain all the resources needed. Confirm that the person knows (a) he or she is making a promise to you, (b) the two of you now have an agreement, and (c) you will follow up with the person to support him or her in keeping his or her promise.

Finally, Closure: tell the person you will follow up at a specific time, and then do exactly that. Let the person know that his or her reliability in this matter is important to you, and that if he or she runs into any unexpected difficulties you expect to hear from the person immediately.

The twenty-five managers who implemented these three conversational practices improved the on-time reliability of the people around them in only six weeks. They raised the average reliability to 95%. One manager said, "It took paying more attention than I usually do to work with people this way, but it was worth it in the long run. My job is easier now that people honor their promises."

Jeannette, the inventory control manager in Chapter 1, took a somewhat different approach to the problem of lateness, but with equal effectiveness. She used a combination of Closure, Initiative, and Performance Conversations. "First, I met with the finance team leader and acknowledged that we had been getting late budget information for the last five months. I told her I was not blaming her or her team, and said I was sure it was not intentional, but I made it clear that I wanted to work with her to find a mutually agreeable solution. She acknowledged that the reports were not intentionally late, and seemed surprised to hear about the problems their lateness created for us. She apologized, and we agreed to put those problems in the past."

"The second thing we did was to brainstorm some ways of resolving the problem. Surprisingly, it took us very little time to hit upon a relatively simple solution involving how we schedule things, including when and how to communicate the inventory closeout dates to her team. At the end, we agreed to implement the new scheduling and communication process, and I promised I would provide immediate feedback directly to her if any future reports arrived late. Although it took us several weeks to work the bugs out, we now rarely get anything late."

Improve work quality. You can improve people's work quality by using conversations for Understanding, Performance, and Closure. Quality means different things to different people: accuracy, completeness, and creativity are the three most common interpretations. You cannot assume everyone knows what you mean if you say only, "I want high quality." You need to spell out what you mean, preferably by using a measure or some objective description, so it is clear to all.

In your Understanding Conversations, say what you mean by "quality, " where you will look to find it, and how you will know when you have it. Let people know if there is a measure you will be using and what it is. A brief Q&A session can be helpful to allow people to ask questions and pose suggestions for measuring and improving quality.

In your Performance Conversations, add the measures or specifications for quality to your request: "I request you reduce the error rate by 5% this month, " or "I request you meet or exceed all five quality specifications on the next quarter's deliverables."

Your Closure Conversations should also focus on quality, so people who are trying to improve their work quality will receive useful feedback on where they succeeded and where they missed the target. They also need to be able to provide feedback themselves. When the results are in, debrief with people on the successes and failures to learn what changes will help long-term quality improvements. Some of the issues identified in these Closure Conversations may become initiatives for future actions, but for now, the intent is to determine what worked, what didn't work, and why. Be sure to acknowledge all improvements in quality and to recognize people for them.

Kate, the insurance account specialist we introduced in Chapter 1, used a combination of Understanding, Performance, and Closure Conversations to improve the quality of work she was getting from sales representatives. "At some point I realized the sales representatives may not actually understand what they were doing that was creating problems for us, " she said. "So, I met with a group of them and asked them to explain how they went about compiling the data. I wanted to understand what they did and why. As we got into it, I discovered there were two problems. One was that they didn't really understand what we were asking for on the form, so they either left it blank or put in what they thought we wanted. The second was that I saw ways to make the form easier for them to use."

"I promised them I would make the changes in the form. But I also kept explaining how to complete the existing form until I was certain that they knew what information to provide and why we needed it. They particularly appreciated understanding why we collected the information and how we used it. That helped them make sense of the form in a new way."

"After that meeting, I made it a point to return every form that was inaccurate or incomplete to the sales rep who filled it out. I attached an explanation of why it was being returned. They didn't like that at first, but it worked. We rarely get incomplete or inaccurate information now."

A tip: interrogate excuses. One of the twenty-five managers in the reliability study above learned a useful tip regarding Closure Conversations that we found applies to both late and poor quality work. "When someone does not deliver what he or she promised, you need to 'interrogate the excuse, '" she told us. "Do not just accept whatever the person gives you as a reason. Ask for details about what went wrong. Was our resource planning inaccurate? Did the schedule management fail? Did the person encounter unforeseen problems? Keep going until you are satisfied the other person can see what happened and how he or she might prevent or resolve similar problems in the future. The point is not to place blame, but to discover what was missing, so people can be more reliable in the future."

On a Saturday afternoon, Ernie's wife Liz suggested that they go out to dinner at the Refectory restaurant the following Friday evening. She asked him to make the dinner reservations at 6:30 PM for four people, while she contacted the other couple that would join them there.

Ernie said, "Sure, I'll call and make the arrangements." But he didn't call that night, even though the restaurant was open. Since the Refectory was closed on Sunday and Monday, Ernie didn't bother to call assuming no one would be there. If he had called, he would have discovered that the restaurant takes voice mail reservations and will call you back to confirm them. Ernie also did not check the restaurant's Web site, where he could have made a reservation online. He planned to get a reservation by calling on Tuesday.

But Ernie didn't call on Tuesday. In fact, he did not call until Wednesday evening. Later on Wednesday night Ernie told Liz, "I called the Refectory about Friday night, and it is full except for 9:30 PM, which I didn't take. If you still want to go out, maybe we should go someplace else."

What Ernie told Liz was accurate, but incomplete. He did not acknowledge that he had waited until Wednesday, which likely contributed to not getting reservations. Had he called on Saturday, or left a phone message, or gone to the Web site, those 6:30 PM reservations might still not have been available. But his communication left Liz with the impression that he had done his best and tried all the options. There was no recognition of future ways to take different actions for better results.

What Ernie did happens all the time in organizations: we forget to do something, and when we remember it, it may be too late. Liz did not "interrogate the excuse, " which is probably best for marital happiness. But a manager who is responsible for improving people's performances must take a different approach.

"I called that vendor, " Gerald said. "But he hasn't gotten back to me yet."

Gerald's manager was waiting for price information to add to his inventory purchasing report. He was not going to be passive about getting what he wanted.

"I need that information to take to the management meeting in the morning, he said. "When did you call? Did you try the supervisor? Is there someone else who could get the information for you?"

In this example, Gerald obviously did not understand his manager's urgency in the situation. The manager had not been specific about when or why he needed the information, so his original request was not a strong one. But the manager chose another path to get what he wanted by not accepting Gerald's reason for failure.

It pays to ask questions when people give you a reason why they did not deliver. Have a Closure Conversation to find out what happened. It is a way of holding people accountable and, by the nature of the questions asked, allows them to see that there were other actions available, including asking you for assistance. When people realize that you will "interrogate the excuse, " they will be more likely to consider alternative ways to get things done. It may also help you make stronger requests in order to reduce disappointment.

Improve Work Relationships

Every organization has people who can be difficult and teams that don't work together as they should. Frequently our response to difficult people is to avoid them if we can, and if we can't, at least avoid doing anything that will "set them off." If these methods don't work, we do our best to put up with an unpleasant situation. Unfortunately, none of these approaches does much to improve the situation.

Similarly, when team members do not pull their weight, we may compensate by reassigning (or doing) their work, then complaining about them and the burden they cause for other team members. But this approach doesn't make the team work any better and can actually add to the problem by building resentment and eroding people's trust and confidence in one another.

Complete the Past with Difficult People

Akasha works in an insurance company designing new promotional campaigns and associated materials. For one of her projects, she needed information from Irena in the marketing section. Akasha planned to use an Understanding Conversation to explain what she needed, and follow it with a Performance Conversation to request the information.

When some of her coworkers found out that Akasha had to meet with Irena, they told her she would be better off solving her problem by herself because, "Nobody can work with Irena." Akasha learned that Irena had a reputation for being very competent but difficult to work with. People said she "snaps at you, ""can't be bothered, " and "is uncooperative."

Akasha needed the information, so she called Irena and set an appointment with her. She decided to approach Irena with a Closure Conversation rather than with an explanation or a request. When the time came for the meeting, Akasha introduced herself and thanked Irena for meeting with her. Then she deepened the Closure Conversation.

"Irena, I must confess I am a little apprehensive about this meeting. I have heard you are very good at what you do, and you are a very busy person. I know your work makes it possible for those of us on the promotion team to do a lot of the development work we do. You probably don't get much recognition, but I personally want to thank you for all that you do. I don't want to cause any difficulty for you, so please let me know the best way for us to work together so I can get the information I need for my team."

When Akasha finished speaking, Irena said, "You know, no one has ever thanked me for what I do until now. I have gotten plenty of criticism, but never a 'thanks.' You are the first. I know people talk about me and my attitude, but I get tired of people coming in here with a lot of 'I' in their talk—'I need this,' "I want this'—expecting me to help them. If I don't, they get upset and blame me for being difficult. I guess it makes me kind of bitter and unpleasant at times."

Irena was not tough, uncaring, and uncooperative as portrayed by her coworkers. She took the time to find what Akasha needed, and promised to send her two other supporting documents by the end of the day.

The Closure Conversation can heal old wounds caused by other people in times long past. In this case, it opened a new relationship that was productive and pleasant, and Akasha soon became known as the only one who could work with Irena. Even though Akasha told her coworkers what she did and how well it worked, only one of them took the opportunity to restore her relationship with Irena by having a Closure Conversation.

John, the systems analyst in Chapter 1, took a similar approach using Closure and Performance Conversations in dealing with a difficult person. "We had a few problems we simply could not resolve without assistance from the expert in decision support, " John explained. "It was beginning to cause issues with our clients. We needed his help, so I went to see him."

"I started by saying I had some problems I needed his help with, and that I was reluctant to ask him to support me. I admitted that there were times in the past when I had come to him for help when I hadn't done everything I could to resolve the problem myself. I also admitted that one time my attempts had made the problem worse, but that I had denied it when he asked. He smiled at that, but I apologized for not having told him the truth about that incident and said he had been right for being critical of me. I promised it wouldn't happen again and said I hoped to restore a good working relationship with him."

"I showed him the problem my team had now and listed everything I had done to try to fix it. When I was done talking, he didn't comment on anything I had said, he just started asking me questions about the problem and my solution methods. He gave me a couple of things to try, one of which ended up working. He is never going to be a warm kind of guy, but we have a different kind of relationship now and when I go talk to him, I go well prepared and he knows it."

Pull teams together. Many things can contribute to breakdowns in teamwork. All four types of conversation can be applied, either separately or in combination, depending on the unique situation of the team and the concerns and interests of the team members.

One cause for teamwork breakdowns is that people lose sight of what they are doing or why they are doing it. When you have Initiative Conversations with teams on a regular basis, you keep people in touch with the

A second possible cause for loss of teamwork is that, as projects progress, changes in roles and responsibilities that once were clear can become ambiguous over time. People can become confused or uncertain about who is doing what, when, or how. Even for teams that have been together for a long time, it is worth having Understanding Conversations on a regular basis to ensure that people are clear on assignments and duties.

Moving ideas into action requires Performance Conversations. When team members fail to make good requests and promises, a decline in productivity or communication can lead to resentments or a reduction in mutual trust and confidence. This is most likely to happen on teams that have been together long enough for people to know each other well and assume they do not need to make well-planned requests and promises any more. When you provide support for good Performance Conversations, you help restore team performance.

Closure Conversations allow team members to debrief their progress on projects and to learn what works and what does not. These conversations also allow teams to address and complete the resentments and hard feelings that can arise when some team members fail to perform or there is an accumulation of broken agreements. It is beneficial to schedule regular occasions for Closure Conversations to provide the opportunity for all team members to address issues before they adversely affect team performance.

Anna, the marketing campaign manager in Chapter 1, used the breakdown between Tammy and Milt as an opportunity to restore teamwork. "I was able to get my team back to normal by having several different conversations, "she said.

"First, I had an Understanding Conversation with Tammy, and then Milt, to find out what exactly had happened between them. Although there were plenty of accusations, I was able to find out that Tammy made a critical comment about Milt a few months ago, and it had festered until it finally came to a head in that argument in front of everyone. Once I knew that, I called both Tammy and Milt together for a Closure Conversation and had them apologize to each other: Tammy for making the comment, and Milt for not addressing it with Tammy sooner."

"In the course of that conversation, I learned that the issue between them was made worse by several changes happening around the marketing campaign that we had not addressed as a team. I decided to add two new components to our regular team meeting, and I put them on the agenda. First, I would restate the purpose and intent of the campaign at the beginning of every meeting. Second, we would take a few minutes to review any changes to our original plan for the campaign and the work each of us needs to do. Milt was especially glad to hear this, and he apologized for having pulled himself away from us instead of coming to me directly. We got everyone reconnected to the campaign and to each other, and it has allowed us to act more like a team than a bunch of individuals with issues.

A tip: turn complaints into action, or quash them. We know one manager who posted a sign in her department's break room saying, "Complain only to someone who can do something about it." She said it helped change the department's culture from being somewhat cynical to getting more people engaged in their projects and activities, and finding solutions to their problems instead of complaining about them.

This manager admitted, "I had to say that slogan at every meeting for months. I had to explain it to a few people who didn't understand what it meant. It was hard for people to believe that I was not going to entertain complaints any more. It was worth the trouble, though, because at some point people started taking responsibility. Either they quit complaining or they got into action. The best thing was that people stopped talking about the same negative things day after day."

Complaints are not productive unless there is a commitment to identify the people and the communications that will resolve them. Some complaints are genuine concerns that need to be investigated and cured. Others are only entertaining, but they can quickly infect all workplace conversations unless you stop them, politely but firmly. One way to do this is by making it your policy to turn every complaint into a request for action.

For example, you can say, "You may be right that the bonuses weren't given out fairly. Who is in a position to get that fixed?" This requires being firm about not getting involved in the complaint conversation and insisting the complainer take an action to resolve it in some way. When you are consistent in turning complaints into requests for action, you will reduce the idle complaints that come your way. A variation on this method of deflecting complaints is to tell people that you do not handle complaints for which you are not responsible. For example, you can say, "I am not the person who can resolve your complaint, so it's not something I can afford to spend much time talking about." This response will turn away most complainers, and reduce the likelihood that they will return.

Another way to turn a complaint into action is to have a Closure Conversation, since the basis for the complaint is something that isn't right with the world. When people believe that something is wrong, it can be useful to acknowledge the facts of the matter and determine what will mend the situation: appreciation, an apology, or an amended agreement. These Closure

Conversations may lead to initiatives that will right the wrongs.

"There should be a way for us to find out the status of projects without calling the project leader, " complained Oscar. "Last week we couldn't use the lab, but no one knew why. It turns out that two projects overlapped on some lab resources, and the other project had priority, so we got bumped. The other project leader said that I should have called him, and he would have told me about the conflict. I guess they expect us to contact all project leaders every day to find out if there are any resource conflicts."

Ray, the lab manager, said, "OK, that's what happened. Do you plan to do anything about it, or do you just want to let off some steam?"

Oscar, choosing action over steam-letting, said, "I think there must be a way to prevent this kind of stuff from happening. If I talked to some IT people, maybe we could come up with an idea."

Ray said, "Great. When will you have a draft of a solution? Give me a date, and I will get Smitty to come to a meeting about it. He's the head of project planning, so he can help us find a way to implement something."

Oscar looked at his schedule and said, "It will take me a few weeks. How about Thursday, April 4?"

Ray put the date on his calendar and agreed to meet and review the solution.

Ray turned a complaint into a Performance Conversation in which both he and Oscar made promises for actions or results. We asked Ray what he would have done if Oscar had said he didn't want to take any action, if he just wanted to let off steam.

"I would have told him it was okay to let off steam, " Ray told us. "I might have given him a few minutes to do that, but no more. I am willing to listen to a little venting from time to time, but, once it is vented, I do not want to hear it again. If you aren't going to do something about it, then let it go. I probably also would have pointed out that we will have other project conflicts unless we are willing to do something about it, to make sure he understood that he couldn't complain about it again if he didn't try to fix it."

When you hear a complaint, you can ask for action or turn it away. Anything else will allow complaints to infiltrate and devalue workplace conversations. Talk truly becomes cheap when uncommitted conversations get the same respectful consideration as committed ones.

Expand Your Personal Effectiveness

A study of knowledge workers in New York found that people have an average of eleven minutes in which to do something before they are interrupted.[1] Success takes more than teamwork—it also requires each of us to find the time and resources for actually doing the work to get the results we promised. Most people have more work to do than they have time in which to do it, and many of them think there is not much they can do about either the amount of work or the amount of time they have available.

We can, however, have some influence on the local conditions that affect our jobs. If we look closely, we may find that some of the overwhelm we experience, or the apparent lack of resources and support, is a function of the conversations we are having.

Choose what won't get done. Do you have a work plan or a "to-do" list with some things on it that have stayed there for more than a week? More than a month? Longer? Does your list continue to grow, because you add more items than you cross off? If you are like most people, the answer is "yes!"

Consider what would happen if you told the truth about some of those items, and admitted that there are things on your list that are, in fact, *never* going to get done. You could also admit that some items are just not going to rise to the top of the list in the near future. In fact, the truth is that you plan to keep them unscheduled until someone insists you buckle down and complete them. All of those different types of incomplete items combine to give you that sense of overwhelm, that sinking feeling that you will never get ahead of the waves of work. They are also a clue that you need to clean up your work plans and promises.

You can reduce the sense of overwhelm by having a Closure Conversation with the people to whom you owe "to do's." Talk about the items you suspect might never get done, the ones that you're sure will not get done in the near future, and the ones you really don't want to do at all. The best place to start is with the ones that have been on your list the longest. Why? Because the people you owe them to probably already realize you are not going to do them.

Todd is someone who prides himself in getting things done. But he noticed items on his "to be completed" list that were getting old or not progressing at all. "When I told the truth about the list, " he said, "I realized that some of those old items were for my boss. I decided to get straight with her, so I made an appointment to talk to her about my list. I told her there were things on my list that had not been done and probably were not going to get done now that she had given me some new responsibilities. She surprised me by thanking me for being honest with her. Even though she knew there were things I hadn't done, she appreciated that I owned up to them."

"She asked me to tell her the specifics, so I told her the ones I didn't think I was going to be able to do, and reviewed the ones I knew I could fit into my work schedule. She picked out the ones that really mattered to her and the ones she didn't care about any more. She also took two items off my list and assigned them to another person in our office, which was a relief to me. We spent another few minutes deciding on realistic due dates for everything that was left on the list. Now my list is shorter and includes only the items I am really going to do. If I ever run into the 'messy list' problem again, I will meet with my manager and let her choose which ones she really wants done and which ones I should drop."

Delegate Effectively

Willis always had trouble delegating work to other people. In the past, whenever he delegated a task, the odds were good that the results did not meet his expectations. To solve the problem, he spent time revising or completely reworking the product. "In the end, it would have been quicker and easier for me to do the work myself, " he said.

Recently he told us, "In my most recent performance evaluation my manager said I needed to delegate more work to other people because I have taken on a new responsibility and can't keep doing everything myself. He also reminded me that I am supposed to develop my colleagues' skills for their careers. This is not the first time I've heard this, but delegation is not something I am good at."

Delegation requires the same skills as improving other people's reliability and quality. The solution is also the same: use plenty of Understanding, Performance, and Closure Conversations:

- Make sure the person you are delegating a task to understands *What*you want, *When*you want it, and *Why*you want it, as well as *Who*the person may need to interact with, *Where*to obtain the resources he or she doesn't have, and *How*to do it. This will be a balance of you giving answers and the person's finding things out for themselves. (You want to avoid getting caught in excessive Understanding Conversations).

- Focus on Performance Conversations. Make a good request and get a good promise: ask for what you want, give a deadline, and state your conditions. Make sure the person is clear about what he or she is promising.

- Create closure: follow up and acknowledge the facts of whatever result you get, including what works and what does not. Get to the bottom of excuses, make room for apologies, and show some appreciation.

When Willis looked at the requirements for the four types of conversation, he saw that he did not give many due dates. "I had them in my head, of course, " he told us, "but I didn't realize I wasn't communicating them."

He also learned that he shared a common failing with many managers, in that he spent very little time having people understand their assignments. Many managers are oriented toward performance, wanting to deliver results as quickly as possible. Willis disliked giving detailed directions or answering questions, feeling it "wastes valuable production time." He discovered it does not.

Without sufficient understanding, people focus on following whatever directions they have without really knowing where they are going. One of Willis's team members told us, "Working with Willis is like trying to follow the directions for putting together a bike without knowing we are building a bike, or even seeing a picture of the bike. It's maddening for us, and he usually doesn't get a very good bike."

Delegation also requires debriefing after the fact. Without Closure Conversations, we miss the chance to improve people's ability to do better next time. "Discuss, request, debrief, " Willis said. "That's my new recipe for delegation, and it works. Although I still have plenty to do, I am not redoing other people's work. As a result, I have more time to do the work I really need to be doing." His next performance review should reflect his improved delegation skills.

Obtain resources by promising results. Most people want more support and more resources to get their work done. Maybe they want a bigger budget, more staff, or new and better equipment, but almost everybody wants something. Too often, when people don't have what they need, they complain to coworkers and struggle to "make do" with what they have. In many cases, however, Performance Conversations can be deployed to obtain additional resources.

Dana is a successful manager who was running up against her resource limits. During the last year, she exceeded her revenue goals by over $70, 000 while other parts of the organization were less successful. She was clear that she could produce even more revenue, but not without an assistant to support her. The problem was that even though Dana was successful, her organization was barely meeting budget and had no funds available for hiring someone.

The approach Dana initially considered taking was to use an Understanding Conversation and explain to her boss all the different tasks the new person would perform and how this would free Dana up to work on other, more revenue-enhancing activities. Dana felt that once he understood the value, he would approve her request. At first blush, this seemed like a good approach. Then Dana considered what her approach would look like from her boss's point of view.

"When I looked from his perspective, " she said, "I suddenly realized that everybody probably takes this approach. I also realized it could make me look like some kind of victim who is overloaded with too much to do. Everyone in the organization could make the exact same argument. So why should he accept my request and not anyone else's?"

Dana had a good point. Her boss was in a position to grant more resources, which meant he would get overloaded himself just trying to deal with people asking for more money, people, and time. Bosses get tired of dealing with people who have complaints instead of solutions, and are likely to respond to them by saying "no."

From the resource holder's standpoint point, everyone is asking for something, but no one is saying what the person will deliver if he or she gets what he or she wants. "So what if I give you this resource?" the person might say. "It will help you, but what will it do for me? You think it will get us more revenue, but how much more, and how soon? Nobody ever tells me about that."

Dana decided she needed to make hiring a new assistant a good investment for her boss. She had historical data that showed whenever she spent more time personally supporting the customer relationships on revenue-generating projects, there was a corresponding increase in revenue in that area. Dana saw she could make the case to her boss that with a new assistant she would be able to generate enough new revenue to not only cover the assistant's salary and benefits, but to also add more to the organization's bottom line within eight months. She could demonstrate a positive return on the hire using data she had in her existing organizational files.

"Armed with this data, " she said, "I met with my boss. I started right out with my request for a new staff person. I then promised that if he accepted my request, I would manage the new hire in such a way that within eight months I would generate enough new revenue to cover the new person's salary plus add to the organization's overall bottom line. I also promised that if I failed to do that, I would relinquish the assistant for use elsewhere in the organization. He accepted my request, and my department is on target for keeping my promise."

A tip: do not assume they know. The single best tip for improving your personal effectiveness at work or at home is to use the conversations that produce results instead of assuming that everyone knows what you know. We have seen hundreds of students and clients, after recovering from the disappointment of realizing that they alone are responsible for every aspect of their own effectiveness, get into action and support the people around them in delivering good results. Communication is at the heart of personal effectiveness, and when we learn to use productive conversations, we can improve our ability to produce results of all kinds. As Willis said, "Discuss, request, debrief."

More Ways to Keep Things Moving

When productivity declines, projects get stuck, and tasks drift off track, we can be sure that one or more of the four conversations has not been used appropriately. People are busy, schedules are overbooked, and anyone who wants a result will have to take responsibility for engaging the partnership and support the person needs for success. You can apply the four conversations to get stuck things moving again. Here are four more tips to restore momentum and pick up speed.

1. **Return to the initiative.** When productivity slows down, or there are setbacks on the way to a goal, people lose focus, become distracted by problems, or overwhelmed by unfinished items. People may not have a clear idea of what to do next. When things are going wrong, results are unfavorable, or mistakes are piling up, it is time to stop the action and return to your purpose.

If the breakdown is large or complex, it may be necessary to update the plan, the action steps, or the timeline. Those options are often not visible from the midst of adversity. Remind yourself of what you set out to accomplish, tell the truth about where you are, without wishful thinking, and update your commitment to the initiative or to your promise. These actions can help you identify the best people with whom to restart the other three productive conversations.

2.

All progress is a function of our conversations. If you are not getting the progress you want or need, it may be time to shift the conversation. Trying to get everyone to understand can be counterproductive, as Denise observed. But people can also get in a rut of overusing other conversations. For example, there are the "idea people" who keep coming up with new things to do and never see them through to implementation. There are "performers" who persist in driving others to make promises for action without taking the time to engage or develop them. And there are "appreciators" who cheerfully praise everyone without giving them good direction or helping them focus on skill improvement for a greater workplace contribution.

The CIO in a large hospital system had a "go live" deadline for a new information system. The project would complete the hospital's integration with a recently acquired smaller hospital in the community. She knew the conversion project was already several weeks behind schedule and feared it might continue falling further behind as they approached the deadline.

At her project management meetings, the CIO listened as her team leaders detailed the problems they were having with system conversion. Each team leader identified one or more problems, giving detailed explanations of the more serious ones. During each presentation, other members raised questions that revealed even more potential problems, which now had to be investigated before the next meeting. The meeting conversation was all about finding and discussing problems.

Concerned about the slow rate of progress, the CIO changed the meeting format and sent an email to all the team leaders, asking that they recommend at least one possible solution for every problem they reported at the next meeting. "I want to hear the problems you are facing, "she told them. "But I also need to hear what you think will solve them. We can no longer afford the time to do so much problem solving in our weekly meetings."

From that point forward, each member presented his solutions and identified the decisions needed to solve the problem. Some of the people on the team were the people who could make the decisions, so some issues were quickly resolved on the spot. If an outside person was the decision maker, the CIO or one of the team members went to them for the decision.

Within six weeks, the number of solutions implemented exceeded the number of new problems identified. At thirteen weeks, the project was almost entirely back on schedule. The CIO said, "Investigating, discussing, and understanding a problem seems like taking action, but nothing really moves until something is implemented. We stopped talking about just problem and started talking about solutions. It's so obvious now, but I couldn't see it for a long time." She was able to rescue a project in trouble, and ultimately meet the go live date.

3.

Two things alter the rate of progress toward any goal: (1) the frequency with which you make requests, and (2) the magnitude of what you ask for. If you maintain all other productive conversations properly, the more frequent and bigger your requests, the faster things will happen. If you increase the number of requests, say from one a day to two a day, you immediately double the number of opportunities for actions or results. When you ask for more action or better results, you similarly increase the opportunities for performance improvements. Asking your sales staff to make seven telephone calls before lunch instead of the usual five will bump up the action, the opportunities, and the potential results. Of course, these requests are fruitless if you fail to spell out the *What-When-Why,* arrange for appropriate skills and other resources, and use the other three types of conversations as needed.

People are often reluctant to ask for more. The child who wants more ice cream could be a useful role model for us in this matter because he or she does not give up. Children are little masters of frequent and bold requests, and they have learned the benefits of doing so. If you learn to make more or bigger requests, more often, to more people, you too will see more actions and more results in a shorter time. Some people may think you are being illogical, pushy, or demanding, but if you want to add velocity to the situation, don't be afraid to ask for whatever ice cream you think will pick up the pace.

4.

When your work reaches a milestone, make it a regular practice to debrief what happened. Identify what worked, what did not, and what everyone can learn from that. Recognize and appreciate what people have done. However tempting it may be to dwell on what might have happened if some things had gone some other way, it is not a good investment of your time. A little second-guessing, or 20/20 hindsight, may offer a lesson for the future, but you are better off using your debrief meeting to review events and facts without making anybody defensive.

It is important to debrief successes as well as failures. Debriefing successes lets you see why you were successful: was it luck or brilliance? You might find some actions you can develop into routines and use to support success in the future.

Putting It into Practice

Knowing which conversations to use, when, and how, will improve with practice and experimentation. This chapter has attempted to answer the question, "How do I determine which conversation I should use?" Although there is no way to answer this question completely without knowing details of a specific situation, some additional guidelines may help you determine which conversation to try.

Situation	Try This First	And Then This
People are not doing what they said they would do when they said they would do it.	Initiative Conversation—review the intended objectives and timelines, and the importance of a positive outcome. Understanding Conversation—have a Q&A session to identify the issues.	Performance Conversation—make requests and promises to resolve the issues. Closure Conversation—follow up to review the results and amend agreements to keep moving ahead.
People are taking a long time to do things and running over deadlines.	Review the Performance Conversation—see if your requests included deadlines, if you are getting good promises, and if you have been consistent in your follow-up.	Closure Conversation—acknowledge the late performance and find out what they suggest to shorten the response time.
People are resisting.	Closure Conversation—acknowledge the resistance and ask people what will reduce or eliminate it.	Performance Conversations—make the requests and promises for actions and results they say will reduce the resistance.
People seem confused, uncertain, or unclear even though you have explained things completely.	Performance Conversation—make requests. (If you have really had a good Understanding Conversation, then understanding is not the issue.)	Closure Conversation—acknowledge promises aren't being kept and find out what is really behind the confusion. Amend agreements as needed.

Situation	Try This First	And Then This
People have ideas that others agree with, but none of the ideas get put into action (a common complaint about meetings).	Performance Conversation—make requests and promises. In meetings, don't adjourn until people have made promises and someone has recorded them.	Closure Conversations—acknowledge the results of the actions taken. At subsequent meetings, make follow-up one of the first agenda items.

Table 9

Conversations don't always work the way we would like. We can launch a terrific Initiative Conversation and some people will still be reluctant to believe success is possible. We can have great Understanding Conversations, and some people will remain unconvinced. We can make rigorous requests and get good promises, and some people will still fail to perform. We can apologize for our mistakes, but some people won't forgive us and will continue to make us pay in some way.

There is no guarantee that any particular conversation will get you all the results you want every time. But

Chapter Seven

Support the Conversational Workplace

The types of conversation you have with the people around you will have a profound impact on your experiences, relationships, and accomplishments. Contrary to the cliché, talk is not cheap. It is a major way of connecting with others and plays a starring role in the quality of your life and the lives of those around you.

Complainers, gossips, and critics talk about what is wrong, who is to blame, and who should fix it. Even if you are a naturally cheerful person, joining a conversation like that will take off the shine. It is difficult to get things done in a place where people are resentful, disengaged, and dissatisfied.

Alternatively, your conversations can support people's engagement, accomplishments, and success. As you have seen throughout this book, it is possible to alter the results you get by making relatively small changes in your conversational patterns. You can improve the performance of others, restore relationships, and enhance your own productivity and effectiveness—all by increasing your skills with the four conversations.

The Conversational Workplace

Our offices, factories, and businesses are conversational workplaces where what people say determines what gets done and how people feel about it. Our conversations build and maintain the culture, set the tone or climate, and create morale and relationship. Nothing gets done in an organization without someone, somewhere, having at least one conversation to get it started, and then lots of other people talking to get it completed. That is the power of conversations.

Initiative Conversations create a future worth achieving. When we set a goal of any kind, we create a possibility of a new future that we believe is worth accomplishing. Our conversations can enroll other people in seeing the possibility and the value, by making the proposed future attractive enough to pull people forward instead of trying to push or manipulate them into action.

Understanding Conversations build trust and relationships. We can include and engage more people in working toward a goal by asking for their input to help develop and improve the plan of action. Engaging people in creating the goals and plans will expand the circle of people who consider themselves an important part of an important endeavor.

Performance Conversations support commitment and accountability. Making requests and promises are the parts of our conversations that serve as levers for performance. They create specific opportunities for people to express themselves, commit to take actions, and produce outcomes and resources. Our conversations clarify responsibilities, show people that accountability begins the moment we say "yes" to a request, and remind us of the value of giving our word to another person.

Practices to Support the Conversational Workplace

Whenever we are in the midst of having a conversation, it is usually so real for us that we are sure we will remember everything about it. In fact, we forget most of what we see and hear, including those very real conversations. Because they are fleeting, we need supports to remind others and ourselves about the details of our conversations, including:

- What have we initiated, when do we want it fulfilled, and why does it matter?
- Who else is engaged in the initiative, where are the resources, and how will everything get done?
- What have we promised, and what have others promised to us?
- How can we observe our progress, remember the most important milestones and deadlines,

and know what needs our follow-through or attention?

Create Visual Reminders: Performance Scoreboards and Other Displays

The saying "What gets measured is what gets done" is not quite accurate. If we keep the measures secret, nobody will know what the score is. Perhaps the more appropriate statement is "What gets measured and talked about is what gets done."

The idea of "visual control" is that we can maintain, and even improve, good performance by making performance visible. The challenge is deciding what is performance. Do you measure everything, or just a few critical things? Should you post a scoreboard on the wall, or is it sufficient to email copies of weekly and monthly results? There are many ways to make performance visible. We have seen all of the following examples:

- Excel spreadsheets on a conference room wall, showing each performance measure with the name of the person accountable for results
- Photos of successful equipment installations, with a statistic showing what percent of each month's results met the success criteria
- Bar graphs, like the United Way thermometer, showing how high the goal is and how much has been accomplished to date

- Collage-like displays of customer letters and success stories that show a team's achievements toward improving customer satisfaction ratings
- Trend-line graphs, showing the changes in results over time
- Bulletin boards listing projects, status, milestones, and resource assignments

The idea is to make the ultimate goal visible and show progress toward reaching it. The effectiveness of this type of performance display depends on regular updates to keep the information current. Just like a sports arena scoreboard, the display of simple statistics keeps everyone engaged in the action, knowing when to cheer and when to take a break.

When we can see the scoreboard, it becomes a topic of conversation. Making performance public and observable is a way to make silent requests, because people can look at the board, see what is needed next, and take action without being told. This principle, of course, works as well at home as it does in the office. A visible schedule of events, or list of chores, can remind us of our household activities and obligations.

Walter, a vice president for financial services of an insurance company, had a very successful service unit, meeting targets more than 95% of the time. He initiated a new goal to reach at least 99%, but he had been unable to get his team engaged. Two of his team leaders said they were satisfied with 95%, and that the amount of work it would take to get beyond that would be too much.

Walter decided not to press the issue, but he posted his service unit's performance on a special bulletin board outside his office and, updated it every week. Since his office was near the entrance to the unit, it was very public, and it was the first thing anyone coming into the unit saw. As a result, people started commenting on, and asking questions about, the unit's performance.

He also added a new item to his weekly staff meeting, asking whether anyone saw something that could be done to improve performance. His staff members began bringing a few more ideas or suggestions to each meeting. Soon they were testing out their ideas before they brought them up in the meeting, so they had more confidence in the value of the improvement.

The net effect of these two changes—a unit performance scoreboard and a new item on the meeting agenda—was that it increased the amount of conversations people had about moving the success rate up higher than 95%. People kept an eye on the scoreboard, and when performance reached 97%, staff members began saying that the 99% goal might be possible. Some people launched new initiatives based on suggestions from the meetings, and others made more requests and promises. One associate invented little celebrations for the wins, and the manager added an item on the agenda to debrief the setbacks when suggestions didn't work. People from other units began to stop by to see what was happening, and soon everyone in the company knew about the 99% goal. Five months later, they hit 99% for the first time.

Track Requests and Promises

What have you promised to deliver to someone else? What has he or she promised to deliver to you? Keep track of these things on a "due" list. A due list is different from a "to-do" list because it identifies the deliverable you are responsible for providing to or receiving from someone else, and it names the other person with whom you have the agreement. In a busy world, you can maintain a due list and match it to your calendar so you know when to expect things and how to schedule doing the work for everything you have to deliver.

Yvette, a system installer with a telecommunications company, prided herself on keeping her promises. She was very good at doing what she said—usually before the due date—except on Fridays.

"Most people look forward to Fridays, " Yvette said. "I don't. Fridays are tough for us. It is a go-go day and we are frequently late to appointments and getting installations done.

There have been more late nights at work on Friday than any other day, but I'm not sure why that is."

She couldn't figure out what it was about Friday that created such a problem for her. Then she created a "due schedule" in which she recorded on her calendar all the things she had promised to deliver and all the things that other people were turning over to her.

"That's when I saw that most things were due on Friday, " she said. "No wonder I was having such a hard time. I had no idea I was doing this to myself. I'm going to start asking people to turn over some of these things earlier. I want more time to pull my deliverables together to avoid being so rushed. My goal is to leave work at 5:00 PM on Fridays like everyone else."

Two weeks after she started using her calendar to keep track of all her "dues, " Fridays were no longer the worst day of the week.

Tracking requests and promises gives you an opportunity to manage your own work better, and to be appropriately responsive to other people. When you know the status of what you owe others—and what others owe you—you also know more about what you can promise and how to make requests that are more effective. This improves both your Performance Conversations (you know when you need to ask for things) and your Closure Conversations (you know when to follow up). The outcome is an increase in your performance and credibility.

Make Meetings Useful: Develop a Standard Agenda for Four Conversations

One of the reasons many people believe meetings are a waste of time is because most meetings are not designed to manage conversations. A well-designed meeting is organized to produce specific results and needs an agenda that will establish the sequence and flow of what is talked about in order to produce those results. Every meeting can open with answers to the three questions that set people up for performance:

- *What* do we want to accomplish? Review your mission, project goals, or objectives for the meeting, so people know the context of the conversation.

- *When* do we want it fulfilled? Remind people of the timelines and milestones associated with the subject of the meeting so they can participate with an awareness of their own calendar and commitments.

- *Why* is it important? Remind people frequently about the value of their work and the meeting.

A meeting that answers these questions will point attention, and subsequent conversations, toward the desired future. You can design the down-to-business portion of the meeting using the four conversations, which makes the meeting easier to facilitate. The result is a standard agenda that you can customize for any meeting.

Initiatives—a Project-Task-Outcome list. What are our outstanding initiatives, goals, and tasks? Are they progressing on schedule? How does each relate to the larger goals of the group?

We have seen many Initiative meeting displays and managers report that they are valuable to help steer their meeting conversations. One generic format shows people everything that is currently in development:

Project-Task-Outcome	Priority (relevance to larger goals)	Person Responsible	Next Milestone/Due Date
1			
2			
3			

Table 10

Understanding—a time to clarify. Every meeting needs a time for people to ask questions or clarify whatever has happened since the last meeting, including reports on progress and changes in people's goals, roles, and responsibilities. This question and answer time is important: if you dismiss or skip over people's questions, you can contribute to creating a culture of "we have to get it done, " or a state of perpetual emergency. Use a Project-Task-Outcome list to keep the conversation on track. Understanding Conversations in meetings help people adjust to changes in plans, activities, or budgets, and they support relationships among team members.

Closure—boasts and leftovers. One standard meeting agenda is to review what has happened with all the promises that were made at prior meetings. When people report on the status of promises, whether they were successful or not, it reinforces their accountability. The meeting becomes the place where promises are completed, redefined, and rescheduled. This may also open up new ideas, returning people to proposing new initiatives.

Boasting is another form of closure. Before you close a meeting, you can ask people if they want to say something about what they have accomplished. When you add a boasting opportunity to your meeting agenda, you encourage people to say something that they are proud of, have completed, or solved. They can also recognize the contributions of others. This conversation teaches people to recognize themselves and each other, and supports future collaboration.

Leftovers can get cleaned up in a Closure Conversation. In every workplace, there are old business practices, documents, and tasks that have become outdated but never cancelled. We know one manager who, when launching a new initiative, starts out with a Closure Conversation. "I want to get the leftovers from past projects out of the way, " he tells everyone. "Clean up your paper and electronic files from the last project." He says people never think to do the cleanup unless he makes it a point to ask them for it. You don't need to wait until a project or task is over to clean up the leftovers from prior projects. You can do it at the end of every meeting.

Implementing the Practices: Four Tips

It is easy to blame problems, barriers, and failures on other people or outside circumstances. It is much more difficult, and takes a bit of courage, to look to our own communication as a contributing factor. The examples in this book, however, illustrate that our patterns of communication do have an impact on the results we get. When you are ready to change your communication style and pattern, here are four tips to help you get started.

1. Tell People You are Changing Your Talk

When you intend to add a new type of conversation, or strengthen it by adding more elements to your existing conversations, it may come as a surprise to some of the people around you. It is not always necessary, but sometimes useful to let them know that you are changing a few things about the way you communicate. Here are some ways we have heard people tell their coworkers or staff members that they are updating their communications:

- "I am going to start setting goals for this team. I plan to be more specific about what we want to accomplish and set schedules and due dates for results. I'll start keeping a list on our whiteboard, including who is assigned to each goal, so we all can see what's happening."

- "Wednesday lunch hours are now on my schedule to eat in the cafeteria. I want to be available to talk with any of you about our projects and problems. Starting this week, I invite any of you to join me for lunch at the big table by the windows, and tell me how things are going with you or your work assignments."

- "I have not been setting up strong agreements with you on your projects, and I need to start doing that. From now on, whenever I assign you a task, I will be talking with you about the milestones of and the resources for doing each job or project. It will help me if you bring your schedules with you when we have our meetings."

- "This is my first week working with this team. I would like each of you to make a list of all the things you are working on, and all the things that are still open or active from the past. In order to start off well in working with you, I need to know what you are carrying over from the previous manager. I will schedule a one-on-one meeting with each of you to review your list and see what we want to keep doing and what you are ready to complete."

2. Play With Your Conversational Patterns

You can learn more about your current pattern of talk by doing some investigative work on your own. Hundreds of managers and MBA students have done an exercise of keeping a diary of their conversations for two weeks. You can do that, or ask your colleagues which of the four conversations they think you use the most and the least. You may also have a collection of emails to and from people, and a little time reviewing them will let you see which types of conversations are the strongest and weakest parts of your communication toolkit.

No single pattern of conversation will serve you in every situation. You are better off trying different conversations with different people, and seeing what happens. The more you are willing to experiment, the more effective you will become.

3. Practice the Hard Parts

Whatever your conversational strengths, there are bound to be some types of conversation that you need to develop. We suggest you practice the ones that are least familiar to you, and start adding the conversational elements you usually omit.

- When you develop your ability to have Initiative Conversations, you are building a greater capacity for leadership and service
- Getting better at Understanding Conversations will make you a better listener and gain you more support and collaboration for projects
- Practicing Performance Conversations will add rigor and clarity to your communications and will make you a better supervisor, team leader, or manager
- Gaining expertise in Closure Conversations will give you an accelerator for resolving people problems and getting more work done with fewer burdens
- Including *What-When-Why* conversational elements in your conversations will give people a context and help them align their intentions with yours
- Including the

When you discover which conversations you need to practice, try using them in a variety of ways and places. Like building a muscle, developing expertise with your conversational patterns takes time and attention, and the payoffs are worth the investment.

4. Tone and Timing Matter

You may not notice the particular tone and manner you have when you talk with people. Maybe you are brusque, even to the point of rudeness, or maybe you are gentle and generous with people. Your own personal tenor is often transparent to you, but the people around you notice it every day.

You can ask yourself (or other people) a few questions about the way you communicate. Do you tend to dictate to people, make demands, and give commands? Are you sarcastic, cynical, or critical? Do you complain that you are mistreated or that your situation is unfair? If any of these are even slightly true for you, that tone will be distracting to people when you are trying to communicate more productively. You can learn to listen, stop complaining, or take more responsibility for the way you operate in your workplace. The benefits will be increased respect and responsiveness from everyone around you.

Timing matters as much as tone. When you have a communication to deliver, make sure you and your audience are able to give it the attention it deserves—stop doing other things. Contrary to popular belief, the brain does not multitask.[1] Those of us who have learned to multitask are really just switching our attention rapidly from one thing to another. When someone you work with, for example, is in the middle of a complicated task, or is troubled or upset, it is probably not the time to make a request or explain a goal. When people are worried, fearful, or angry, they are distracted and may not be able to interact effectively, much less remember whatever promises they say they will keep.

A Closing Note

Conversations are everywhere, and they don't all have to be serious or productive. Conversations that are frivolous, creative, or romantic are fine, and our lives are richer for them. Life is not all about being productive, but improving our conversational skills may help us avoid being counterproductive, which is all good.

Changing the way you conduct certain conversations is much more than just rearranging words or asking new questions. Your conversations are a vital ingredient in the quality of your life. When you bring more attention to the quality of your conversations, you interact more thoughtfully and respectfully. We expect this will help you reach your goals as you help others reach theirs, and we hope you reap the benefits in your environment, your relationships, and your personal satisfaction and success.

Resources

The following are just a few of the books that will help you in developing further your ability to use the Four Conversations.

Adams, Marilee. *Change Your Questions, Change Your Life: 7 Powerful Tools for Life and Work.* San Francisco: Berrett-Koehler, 2004.

The Arbinger Institute. *Leadership and Self-Deception: Getting Out of the Box.* San Francisco: Berrett-Koehler, 2002.

Bridges, William. *Managing the Transitions: Making the Most of Change, 2nd Ed.* Cambridge, MA: Da Capo, 2003.

Canfield, Jack, Mark V. Hansen, and Les Hewitt. *The Power of Focus.* Deerfield Beach, FL: Health Communications Inc., 2000.

Isaacs, William. *Dialogue and the Art of Thinking Together.* New York: Doubleday Currency, 1999.

Kador, John. *Effective Apology. Mending Fences, Building Bridges, and Restoring Trust.* San Francisco: Berrett-Koehler, 2009.

Kouzes, James M. and Barry Z.Posner. *Credibility: How Leaders Gain and Lose It, Why People Demand It.*San Francisco: Jossey-Bass, 1993.

Scott, Susan. *Fierce Conversations: Achieving Success at Work and in Life, One Conversation at a Time.* New York: Viking, 2002.

Stone, Douglas, Bruce Patton, and Shelia Heen. *Difficult Conversations: How to Discuss What Matters Most.* New York: Viking, 1999.

Tannen, Deborah. *Talking from 9 to 5: Women and Men at Work.* New York: Quill, 2001.

Ventrice, Cindy. *Make Their Day! Employee Recognition that Works.* San Francisco: Berrett-Koehler, 2003.

Wagner, Rodd and James K. Harter. *12: The Elements of Great Managing.* New York: Gallup Press, 2006.

Yankelovich, Daniel. *The Magic of Dialogue: Transforming Conflict into Cooperation.*New York: Simon and Schuster, 1999.

Notes

Preface

[1]   Michael Beer, Russell Eisenstat, and Bert Spector. "Why change programs don't produce change."*HarvardBusinessReview,*November–December, 1990, p. 158–166; John Kotter. "Leading Change: Why Transformation Efforts Fail." *Harvard Business Review,*March–April, 1995, p. 59–67; Nitin Nohria. "From the M-Form to the N-Form: Taking Stock of Changes in the Large Industrial Corporation" (Harvard Business School Working Paper 95-054).

Chapter 1

[1]   Douglas Stone, Bruce Patton, and Sheila Heen. *Difficult Conversations: How to Discuss What Matters Most.* New York: Viking, 1999.

Chapter 2

[1]   Warren Bennis and Bert Nanus.
[2]   Timothy Gallwey. *The Inner Game of Work.* New York: Random House, 1999, p. 43.
[3]   Lawrence G. Shattuck. "Communicating Intent and Imparting Presence, " *Military Review,*Mar–Apr. 2000, pp. 66–72.

Chapter 3

[1]   Rodd Wagner and James K. Harter. *12: The Elements of Great Managing.* New York: Gallup Press, 2006, p. 112.
[2]   Ibid, p. 111.

[3]   Kurt Dirks, Larry Cummings, and Jon Pierce. "Psychological ownership in organizations: Conditions under which individuals promote and resist change." In R. W. Woodman and W. A. Pasmore (eds.), *Research in Organizational Change and Development Volume 9.* Greenwich, CT: JAI Press Inc., 1996, pp. 1–23.

[4]   Jeffrey Pfeffer and Robert I. Sutton. "The Smart-Talk Trap." *Harvard Business Review,*May–June, 1999, pp. 134–142.

[5]   Michael Beer, Russell Eisenstat, and Bert Spector. "Why Change Programs Don't Produce Change." *Harvard Business Review,*November–December, 1990, pp. 158–166.

Chapter 4

[1]   Cited at http://www.mylifecoach.com/are_you _stuck_answers.html.

Chapter 5

[1]   Dan Strutzl. "The Unvarnished Truth." www.advantedgemag.com, July–August, 2006, pp. 72–73.

[2]   Rodd Wagner and James K. Harter. *12: The Elements of Great Managing.* New York, Gallup Press, 2006, p. 52

[3]   Del Jones. "It's not just lonely at the top; it can be 'disengaging, ' too." *USA Today,*June 20, 2005.

[4]   Cindy Ventrice. *Make Their Day! Employee Recognition that Works.* San Francisco, CA: Berrett-Koehler, 2003.

[5]   John Kador. *Effective Apology: Mending Fences, Building Bridges, and Restoring Trust.* San Francisco, CA: Berrett-Koehler, 2009.

[6]   James Kouzes and Barry Posner. *Credibility: How Leaders Gain and Lose It, Why People Demand It.*San Francisco, CA: Jossey-Bass, 1993.

[7]   Carrie Ghose. "'Sorry' laws build on slow shift to honesty, " *Business First,*Columbus, OH: November 23, 2007, pp. B1, B3.

[8]   James Q. Wilson and George L Kelling. "Broken Windows, " *Atlantic Monthly,*March 1982, pp. 29–38.

[9]   An empirical test of the broken windows theory is provided by Hope Corman and Naci Mocan "Carrots, Sticks, and Broken Windows, " *Journal of Law and Economics,*April 2005, 48:1: pp.235–266.

[10]   Ellwood Oakley and Patricia Lynch. "Promise-keeping. A Low Priority in a Hierarchy of Workplace Values." *Journal of Business Ethics,*27:4, October 2000, pp. 377–392. In a study of 700 managers and students, Oakley and Lynch report that promise-keeping consistently ranked last in a hierarchy of workplace values. Even with the possibility

of legal sanctions, fewer than one-third of the subjects kept their word.

Chapter 6

[1]   Claudia Wallis and Sonia Steptoe. "Help, I've Lost My Focus." *Time,*Feb 6, 2006.

Chapter 7

[1]   John Medina. *Brain Rules: 12 Principles for Surviving and Thriving at Work, Home, and School.* Seattle, WA: Pear Press, 2008.

Acknowledgments

This material comes from the work we have done with thousands of managers, clients, and students in boardrooms, classrooms, and workshops. We are grateful for the problems they have posed to us, their commitment to trying new ways to get things done, and allowing us into their lives. They pushed us to make it easier for them to be more successful, and effective at work and in life. We learned from them, and without them this book would not have been possible.

Although we are solely responsible for the content of this book, many people have contributed their ideas and recommendations. Jacqueline Davis, Carolyn Kent, and Lisa Krumlauf generously reviewed previous drafts of the manuscript and provided detailed comments that made it a better book. Agnes Bourne, Paul Melko, and Blaine Bosley made suggestions and provided ideas about what was missing that would strengthen the final product. We are grateful for their contributions and their hard work.

We are also indebted to the friends and family members who endured our incessant talking about "the book" while providing support and encouragement. Jeffrey's daughter, Danielle, and son, Kyle, were the source of several examples, as was Laurie's sister, Wende Wilson. Our neighbors, Deryl and Lauren Kowalski and Troy and Melissa Wren, cheered us on and were always willing to listen to the progress we were making (or not). We are grateful for their support and willingness to engage in helping us with this project.

We have benefited from the extensive writings in management theory, sociology, psychology, and communication theory, as well as countless professional and trade books. The educational programs and leaders of Landmark Education and the work of Brian Regnier, in particular, have also been instrumental in shaping our thinking, and we thank them for the difference they have made for us.

About the Authors

Jeffrey and Laurie Ford are, both literally and figuratively, a marriage of theory and practice. Jeffrey is an associate professor of management in the Max M. Fisher College of Business at The Ohio State University in Columbus, Ohio. He holds a B.S. in marketing from the University of Maryland, and an MBA and a Ph.D. in organizational behavior from The Ohio State University. Prior to joining Fisher, Jeffrey served on the faculties of the Institute of Management and Labor Research at Rutgers—The State University of New Jersey, and the Kelly School of Business at Indiana University.

Laurie is a management consultant and owner of Critical Path Consultants. She holds a B.S. in psychology, a Master's degree in industrial engineering, and a Ph.D. in operations research engineering, from the State University of New York at Buffalo. Prior to starting her own business, Laurie was a consultant with Arthur Anderson in Washington D.C. Since then, she has served as a consultant to scores of businesses, government agencies, and not-for-profit organizations, including Intel, Mead Paper, U.S. Department of Energy, NASA, the Ohio State Medical Association, and the Ohio Hospital Association. Laurie has also taught graduate-level university courses in engineering, management, and organization design.

Jeffrey likes to say he teaches what Laurie practices, and Laurie says she practices what Jeffrey teaches. Their collaboration has resulted in a unique approach to making management easier and organizational change less painful. Jeffrey's MBA classes, where Laurie is a frequent and popular visitor, are recognized for their unique perspective and immediately usable content, making Jeffrey an award-winning teacher.

Laurie, who has backpacked around the world and motorcycled across the United States, is known for making the difficult happen with surprising ease. A professional speaker and program leader, she has an engineering background that provides her with the powerful tools of network theory. She has used these tools to develop a unique "hotwiring" method to locate and resolve the invisible disconnects between individuals and groups that can limit organizational performance.

Together, Jeffrey and Laurie have coauthored over a dozen articles for academic and professional management journals including the Harvard Business Review. Coauthors of *"Deadline Busting: How to be a Star Performer in Your Organization, "*they also publish the twice-monthly Great Managing Newsletter, free to subscribers.

Jeffrey and Laurie work together, and separately, to deliver conference and in-house programs on their unique approach to management, including effective communications within and between groups, and engaging people in improving productivity and accountability. To talk with Jeffrey or Laurie about delivering a program for your organization, contact Jeffrey at f ord.1@osu.edu and/or Laurie at laurie@laurieford.co m. We also welcome your questions and suggestions about using the Four Conversations at www.usingthe fourconversations.com.

About Berrett-Koehler Publishers

Berrett-Koehler is an independent publisher dedicated to an ambitious mission: Creating a World That Works for All.

We believe that to truly create a better world, action is needed at all levels—individual, organizational, and societal. At the individual level, our publications help people align their lives with their values and with their aspirations for a better world. At the organizational level, our publications promote progressive leadership and management practices, socially responsible approaches to business, and humane and effective organizations. At the societal level, our publications advance social and economic justice, shared prosperity, sustainability, and new solutions to national and global issues.

A major theme of our publications is "Opening Up New Space." They challenge conventional thinking, introduce new ideas, and foster positive change. Their common quest is changing the underlying beliefs, mindsets, institutions, and structures that keep generating the same cycles of problems, no matter who our leaders are or what improvement programs we adopt."

We strive to practice what we preach—to operate our publishing company in line with the ideas in our books. At the core of our approach is *steward-ship,* which we define as a deep sense of responsibility to administer the company for the benefit of all of our "stakeholder" groups: authors, customers, employees, investors, service providers, and the communities and environment around us.

We are grateful to the thousands of readers, authors, and other friends of the company who consider themselves to be part of the "BK Community." We hope that you, too, will join us in our mission.

Be Connected

Visit Our Website

Go to www.bkconnection.com to read exclusive previews and excerpts of new books, find detailed information on all Berrett-Koehler titles and authors, browse subject-area libraries of books, and get special discounts.

Subscribe to Our Free E-Newsletter

Be the first to hear about new publications, special discount offers, exclusive articles, news about bestsellers, and more! Get on the list for our free e-newsletter by going to www.bkconnection.com.

Get Quantity Discounts

Berrett-Koehler books are available at quantity discounts for orders of ten or more copies. Please call us toll-free at (800) 929-2929 or email us at bkp.or ders@aidcvt.com.

Host a Reading Group

For tips on how to form and carry on a book reading group in your workplace or community, see our website at www.bkconnection.com.

Join the BK Community

Thousands of readers of our books have become part of the "BK Community" by participating in events featuring our authors, reviewing draft manuscripts of forthcoming books, spreading the word about their favorite books, and supporting our publishing program in other ways. If you would like to join the BK Community, please contact us at bkcommunity@bkpub.com.

Books For ALL Kinds of Readers

At ReadHowYouWant we understand that one size does not fit all types of readers. Our innovative, patent pending technology allows us to design new formats to make reading easier and more enjoyable for you. This helps improve your speed of reading and your comprehension. Our EasyRead printed books have been optimized to improve word recognition, ease eye tracking by adjusting word and line spacing as well as minimizing hyphenation. Our EasyRead SuperLarge editions have been developed to make reading easier and more accessible for vision-impaired readers. We offer Braille and DAISY formats of our books and all popular E-Book formats.

We are continually introducing new formats based upon research and reader preferences. Visit our web-site to see all of our formats and learn how you can Personalize our books for yourself or as gifts. Sign up to Become A RHYW Registered Reader.

www.readhowyouwant.com

Made in the USA
Monee, IL
06 July 2022

99154712R10168